French Inspirations
for Artful Hands

September days spent traveling the French Countryside
were the inspiration for the quilts and sweet offerings
within our book. Our sincerest wish is that
you enjoy every page of our journey.

Bonnie Sullivan *&* Kathy Schmitz

*Mont Saint-Michel is a rocky tidal
island surrounded by water at high tide.
This was definitely one of our favorite destinations!
We arrived in the late afternoon and watched as
a storm moved in. With thunder and lightening, and
buckets of rain, we experienced a magical Mont Saint-Michel.*

French Inspirations for Artful Hands

A Quilt and Project Book

Authors: Bonnie Sullivan & Kathy Schmitz (Bonnie won Rock, Paper Scissors)

Appliqué: Marjorie McCanse, Margie Bergan, Kathy Schmitz, Bonnie Sullivan

Piecing: Bonnie Sullivan, Kathy Schmitz, Marjorie McCanse & Margie Bergan

Sewing: Bonnie Sullivan & Kathy Schmitz

Machine Quilting: Laurel Keith/Hawn Creek Quilting
Loretta Orsborn/Orsborn Specialty Quilting
Pam Parvin/Kaylee Quilting

Directions: Bonnie Sullivan & Kathy Schmitz

Page Design: Kathy Schmitz

Editing: Bonnie Sullivan & Kathy Schmitz

Photography: Kathy Schmitz, Bonnie Sullivan & Sean Sullivan

Published by Kathy Schmitz and Bonnie Sullivan
First Edition
ISBN:978-0-615-53037-6

Printed in the
United States of America by
Palmer Printing

To order this book go to
www.AllThroughtheNight.net or
www.KathySchmitz.com

Let's go to France someday!

Some of my fondest childhood memories are of times spent crafting with my sisters. Our Mother had set up a space for the three of us girls with all kinds of art materials. We would while away the hours being limited only by our imaginations. I do remember fabrics being one of my favorite mediums to create with and I spent many hours making tiny upholstered doll furniture and Troll clothes.

It wasn't until several years later that I would return to those creative roots that had taken hold so long ago. When my first son was born I decided I wanted to stay home with him, but also knew that I needed to find a way to contribute financially to the family. I began crafting in earnest and selling my creations at local craft fairs.

My creative focus changed around 2001 when I was introduced to working with wool - it gave me that same warm feeling I had of being back in the creative room of my childhood home. I designed a line of Penny Rug patterns and went to my first International Quilt Market with Kathy in the Spring of 2002 in Kansas City. Neither of us really knew what to expect and we met with our suitcases full of samples at the airport, asked each other what we were doing, and took the leap. We haven't looked back since. Soon after that I approached Maywood Studio with some ideas for a fabric line and began working with them in 2003.

While I enjoy my work, raising my two fine sons, Marcus and Sean, has always been my priority and I've so adored watching them turn into the amazing young men they are today. I've long loved the way children experience the world with such curiosity and wonder, and hope that I will remember to view things with that same sense of innocence, imagination, and enthusiasm. What a gift they have given me.

The past few years have afforded me the opportunity to do some traveling overseas and I have found inspiration at every turn and long to further explore this incredible world we live in. When Kathy and I decided to take this journey to France, we went with the idea of letting the trip take us where it would and we were not disappointed. We had so much fun and learned that we traveled very well together - whew!! Working on this book with Kathy has made me appreciate her talents even more. Thank you Kathy for all that you have done to make this dream possible.

Most importantly I would like to thank my family and friends without whose support, encouragement, and understanding it would have been much more difficult to take this trip of a lifetime. Thank you from the bottom of my heart.

Bonnie

Some of my earliest memories included paper & scissors and needle & thread. Whether I was watching my Mom and Grandmothers quilt and create or "creating" something myself, I was hooked at an early age - my hands were happiest when they were busy!

For many years I painted watercolors of Santas, snowmen, houses, chairs with teacups on the arm, and anything else that inspired me. I would sell them at a local craft fair once a year. During the rest of the year I raised my two boys, Cory and Tom, and I would teach art in my their grade school classrooms. Then for some reason, once they hit middle school, it wasn't cool to have their mom at school anymore. I needed another avenue to satisfy my creative soul. In 2002 I decided to turn my love of painting and crafting into a business and I went to my first International Quilt Market selling greeting cards with quilty images on them. It felt like coming home to a house full of fun, and often loud relatives; eager to share their years of experience and sincerely welcoming me into the quilting industry. I brought my portfolio of paintings with me and with all the false bravado I could muster I shared them with Moda. It was a good move on my part; I have been happily designing fabric for them ever since. In 2007, missing that needle and thread in hand, I decided to design embroidery patterns as well. This combination of drawing and stitching was a perfect marriage.

With Bonnie in the same industry, we have shared hotel rooms and laughs, but we thought it was time to work together on a project. We decided if we were going to combine forces we may as well go all out; We needed to go to France! September of 2010 was spent in a magical land full of castles and flea markets (and creme brûlée) where every urn and door knocker inspired a quilt or project.

Working on this book, looking through our treasures and pictures, has been like reliving that French journey all over again. For me, this book is a treasured photo album of our journey, every page a wonderful memory. I hope, with all of my heart, you will share the joy of our trip through these pages.

I live in Portland, Oregon with my husband Steve in a little brick cottage. My sons are young men now and make me proud every day. I am blessed beyond measure. Thank you, Steve, for your support, love and understanding while working on this book and every day of our lives.

Kathy

P.S. Bonnie, thanks for the good time!

Our heartfelt thanks

Thank you Sean Sullivan, Bonnie's son, for your excellent photography on pages 5, 33 and our portrait.
Thank you Erynn Gerber, our beautiful niece, for letting us talk you into modeling our projects on page 33.
Thank you Ann Fenderson, our sister, for creating such beautiful necklaces from the bits and pieces we brought back from our trip. Your creations are so wonderful and we love everything you have every made us.
A special thank you Margie Bergan for your precision piecing on the Brantôme quilt and gorgeous appliqué work on the Ville De Paris quilt. Thank you also for being a trustworthy quilt courier and kindly sharing your time and talent.
Most of all we would like to thank our Mom Marjorie McCanse, for her masterful appliqué work on the Ville De Paris quilt, her impeccable binding work on several of the projects and for all of her encouragement through the years.

Table of Contents

Ville De Paris

Ville De Paris Measures 64" x 64"

Designed by Bonnie Sullivan & Kathy Schmitz
Pieced by Marjorie McCanse
Applique by Marjorie McCanse & Margie Bergan
Quilting by Loretta Orsborn/Orsborn Specialty Quilting

Supplies & Cutting Directions

2 1/2 yards
Cut 2 - 16" strips across width of fabric.
Cut 4 - 6 1/2" strips across width of fabric.
Cut 2 - 3 1/2" strips across width of fabric. Cut 2 - 3 1/2"x 10 1/2" pieces. Cut 2 - 3 1/2 "x 16 1/2" pieces.
Cut 1 - 2 1/2" strip across width of fabric. Cut 12 - 2 1/2" squares.
Draw a diagonal line on the back of 8 of the 2 1/2" squares.
Use the remaining fabric for binding.

1 1/2 yards
Cut 2 - 16" Strips across width of fabric.
Cut 1 - 10 1/2" square and 12 - 2 1/2" squares.

1/2 yard
Cut 3 - 4 1/2" strips across width of fabric. Cut 4 1/2" strips into 24 - 4 1/2" squares.
Cut 36 berries from the remaining fabric.

1 1/8 yards
Cut 4 - 7 1/2" strips across width of fabric. Cut 7 1/2" strips into 18 - 7 1/2" squares.
Cut the bird for appliqué center of quilt and cut 36 berries from the remaining fabric.

A fat 1/4 of each of these fabrics (E through M)
From each fabric - Cut 2 - 7 1/2" squares and 8 - 2 1/2" squares.
Draw a diagonal line on the back of each of the 2 1/2" squares

1/8 yard
Cut 8 - 2 1/2" squares.
Draw a diagonal line on the back
of each of the 2 1/2" squares.

1 1/2 yards
Cut 5 diagonal (bias) strips 1 1/2" wide for vines
Cut 8 - 2 1/2" squares and foliage from
remaining fabric.

5"x 20"
Cut 36 berries.

The Eiffel Tower, Arc-de-Triomphe, the Louvre, and Flea markets were all must sees. From the Eiffel Tower take metro to porte de Clignancourt and follow signs to Marchés aux puces (Flea market)

4 yards - Backing fabric
12 wt Dark Green Perle Cotton

Assembly: (all seam allowances are 1/4" unless otherwise indicated)

1/4" seams are very important in this quilt as they are in any quilt. It is important to make sure that the seams you are taking really are 1/4". You can do this by sewing together 5 - 1 1/2" strips (any length will do). Press the seams open and measure. The finished measurement should be 5 1/2" across.

BLOCKS: There are three different blocks in the piecing of this quilt.

1. The first blocks will be the half square triangle blocks of **A** and **B** fabric. Match a 16" strip of brown (**B**) with a 16" strip of small check (**A**). With right sides together cut 2 1/4" diagonal strips across the whole piece. Now carefully take the diagonal strip sets and sew a seam 1/4" in on both sides making sure not to pull or stretch the edges as they are on the bias. Repeat with remaining 16"strips of brown and small check. Cut 296 - 2 1/2" squares from sewn diagonal strip sets.

2. The next pieced block is the 4 1/2" red block with the snowballed corners (the inside border). For these blocks you will need the 24 - 4 1/2" squares of **C** (raspberry red) and 8 of the 2 1/2" squares of various colors (**A,E,F,G,H,I,J,K,L,M, N & O**). Do **NOT** use the 2 1/2" squares of **B** and four of the 2 1/2" squares of **A**. Randomly choosing your fabric, snowball off the four corners of the red (**C**) 4 1/2" squares as shown - a different fabric on each corner. *Sew an additional seam 1/2" away from the seam used to snowball the corner as shown and cut away the excess fabric. This is an optional step, but it will leave you with 96 additional small half square triangle blocks that you can use to make the framed wall hanging featured on page 72.*

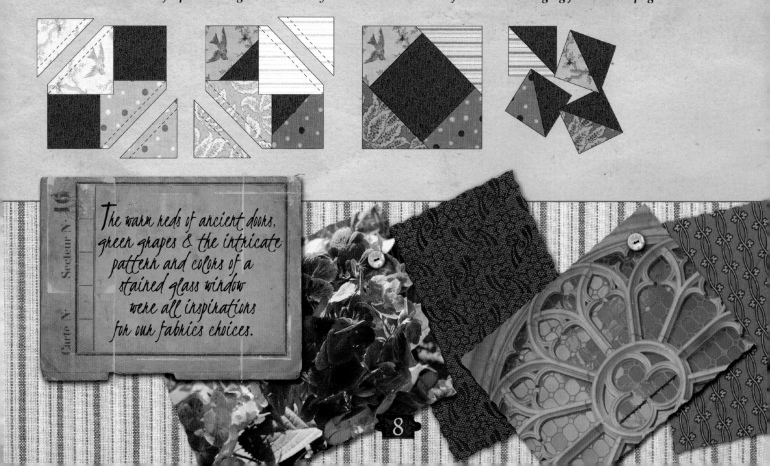

The warm reds of ancient doors, green grapes & the intricate pattern and colors of a stained glass window were all inspirations for our fabrics choices.

3. The third pieced block is the nine patch. For the nine patches you will be using the 18 - 7 1/2" squares of **D** and the 7 1/2" squares of **E,F,G,H,I,J,K,L** and **M.** Match up each 7 1/2" square of **D** with a 7 1/2" square of another fabric.

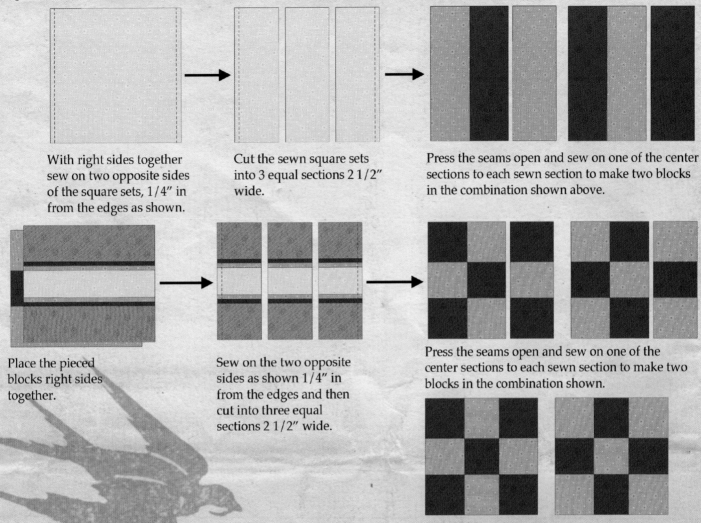

With right sides together sew on two opposite sides of the square sets, 1/4" in from the edges as shown.

Cut the sewn square sets into 3 equal sections 2 1/2" wide.

Press the seams open and sew on one of the center sections to each sewn section to make two blocks in the combination shown above.

Place the pieced blocks right sides together.

Sew on the two opposite sides as shown 1/4" in from the edges and then cut into three equal sections 2 1/2" wide.

Press the seams open and sew on one of the center sections to each sewn section to make two blocks in the combination shown.

PIECING:

Sew the 2 light plaid (**A**) 3 1/2" x 10 1/2" pieces to the top and the bottom of brown (**B**) 10 1/2" square. Press.
Sew the 2 light plaid (**A**) 3 1/2" x 16 1/2" pieces to the two sides. Press

Sew 8 half square triangle blocks together as shown. Press.
Make two of these strips. Sew one to the top and one to the bottom of the pieced center so far. The light half of the sewn strips are toward the center block.

Sew 8 half square triangles together as shown. Sew a 2 1/2" brown square to each end. Make two of these strips and sew them to the sides of the center block, again with the light fabric toward the center block.

IMPORTANT: *Stay stitch a scant 1/4" around the sawtooth border.*

Cut out appliqué pieces in the designated colors.

VINE: Take the 1 1/4" bias strips and fold them in half lengthwise, WRONG sides together. Sew along the raw edge side using a 1/4" seam. Trim the raw edge to a scant 1/8". Press so that the seam, and raw edges run down the center of the vine. *Press very well and let the vines cool completely.*

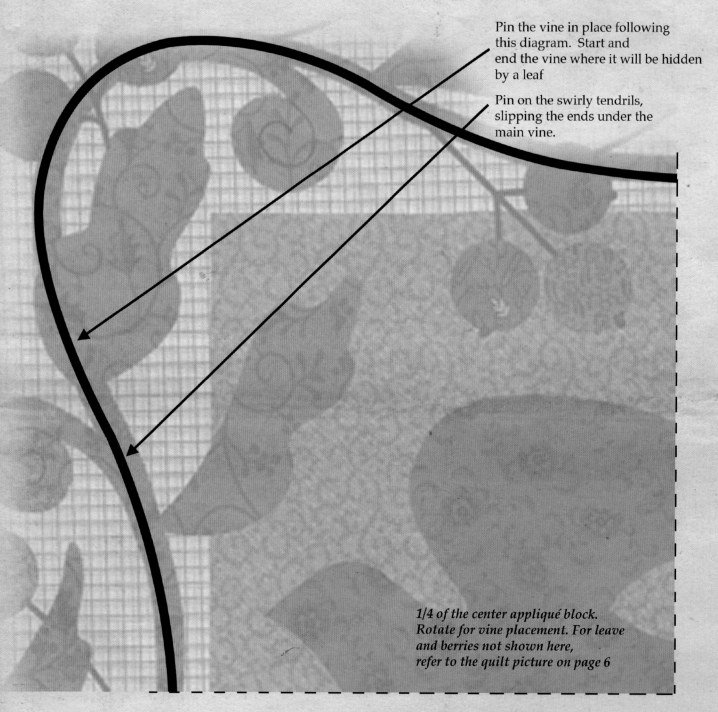

Pin the vine in place following this diagram. Start and end the vine where it will be hidden by a leaf

Pin on the swirly tendrils, slipping the ends under the main vine.

1/4 of the center appliqué block. Rotate for vine placement. For leave and berries not shown here, refer to the quilt picture on page 6

Appliqué the main vine in place. Arrange the leaves and berries following this diagram and the quilt picture on page 6. Appliqué them in place. Appliqué the bird in the center block. Using the Perle cotton, stem stitch the berries to the vine. Add a French knot to the top of each berry. Stem stitch the swirl inside of the tendril. Make an eye on the bird using a black Perle Cotton French knot. Samples of embroidery stitches may be found on page 13.

Sew five snowballed blocks (block 2) together. Sew this strip to the top of the appliquéd center block.
Sew five more snowballed blocks (block 2) together. Sew this strip to the bottom of the appliquéd center block.
Sew seven snowballed blocks (block 2) together. Sew this strip to the side of the appliquéd center block.
Sew the last seven snowballed blocks (block 2) together. Sew this strip to the other side of the appliquéd center block.

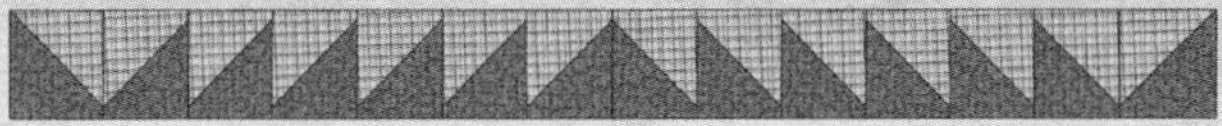

Sew 14 half square triangle blocks together following the diagram. Make two of these strips. Sew these strips to the top and bottom with the brown fabric toward the snowballed blocks.

Sew 14 half square triangle blocks together following the diagram. Sew a 2 1/2" light plaid square to each end. Make two of these strips. Sew these strips to the two sides with the brown fabric toward the snowballed blocks.

Using the 6 1/2" strips of the light plaid (A) cut 2 to 32 1/2" in length. Sew these to the top and the bottom. Take the remaining fabric from the above strips and sew them onto the ends of the last 2 - 6 1/2" strips. Press the seams open. Cut these two strips to 44 1/2". Sew theses strips to the sides.

Sew 22 half square triangle blocks together following the diagram. Make two of these strips. Sew these strips to the top and the bottom with the light plaid fabric toward the quilt center.

Sew 22 half square triangle blocks together following the diagram. Sew a 2 1/2" brown square to each end. Make two of these strips. Sew these strips to the sides with the light fabric toward the quilt center. Stay stitch a scant 1/4" around the entire piece so far.

Down the center of the outside light plaid border, make a small, removable, mark every 6 3/8" - 6 1/2" (5 equal sections) starting and ending straight out from the inside corners. Do this on all four sides.

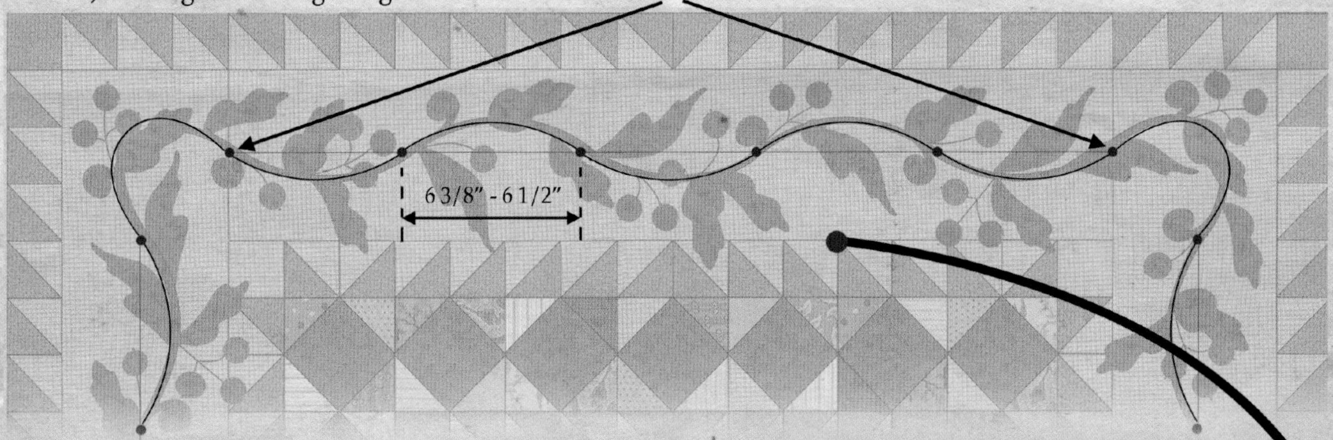

6 3/8" - 6 1/2"

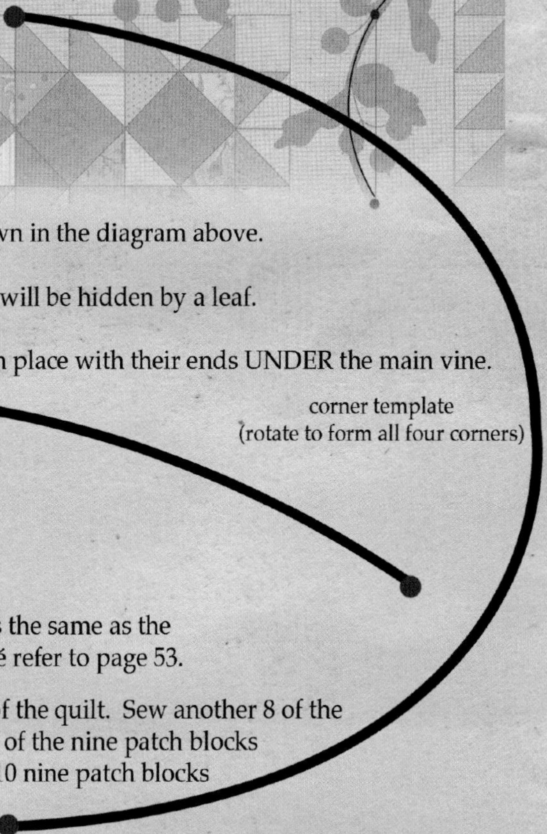

Using these templates, create a wavy pattern for the vine placement as shown in the diagram above.

Pin the vine in place. Start and stop each piece of vine in a corner where it will be hidden by a leaf.

Arrange the swirly tendrils following the diagram above. Appliqué them in place with their ends UNDER the main vine.

Appliqué the vine.

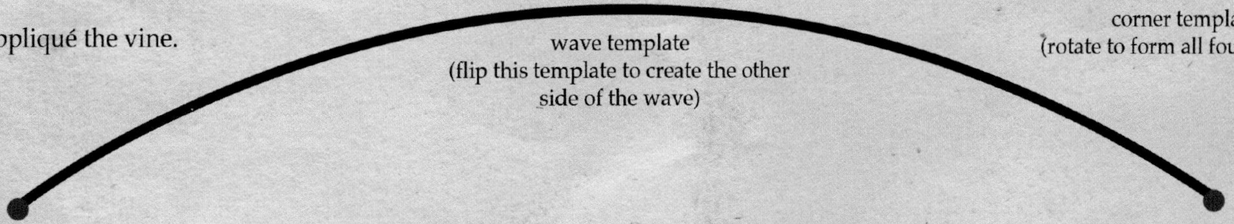

wave template
(flip this template to create the other side of the wave)

corner template
(rotate to form all four corners)

Appliqué the leaves and the berries. Embroider the stems and French knots the same as the inside appliqué border. For a tip on how to make perfect circles for appliqué refer to page 53.

Sew 8 of the nine patch blocks (Block 3) together. Sew this strip to the top of the quilt. Sew another 8 of the nine patch blocks together. Sew this strip to the bottom of the quilt. Sew 10 of the nine patch blocks together. Sew this strip to one of the sides of the quilt. Sew the remaining 10 nine patch blocks together. Sew this strip to the other side of the quilt.

Sew 30 half square triangle blocks together as shown above. Sew this strip to the top of the quilt. Make another one of these strips and sew it to the bottom of the quilt. Sew with the brown fabric toward the nine patch blocks.

Sew 30 half square triangle blocks together as shown above. Sew a 2 1/2" brown square to each end. Sew this strip to a side of the quilt. Make another one of these strips and sew it to the final side. Sew with the brown fabric toward the nine patch blocks.

Quilt and bind. Binding tips on page 53.

O fabric
Cut 12
Cut 12 mirrored
(total of 24)

These patterns do not include seam allowance. Cut fabric a scant 1/4" larger for turned applique. For the berries cut a generous 1/4" larger than the pattern. For fused applique the patterns will need to be reversed.

french knot
with black floss

D fabric
Cut 1

O fabric
Cut 24

O fabric
Cut 16
Cut 12
mirrored
(total 28)

Stem stitch after
applique is sewn in
place.

C, D & P
red fabrics

36
of each

French knot
berry top

O fabric
Cut 16
Cut 8 mirrored
(total of 24)

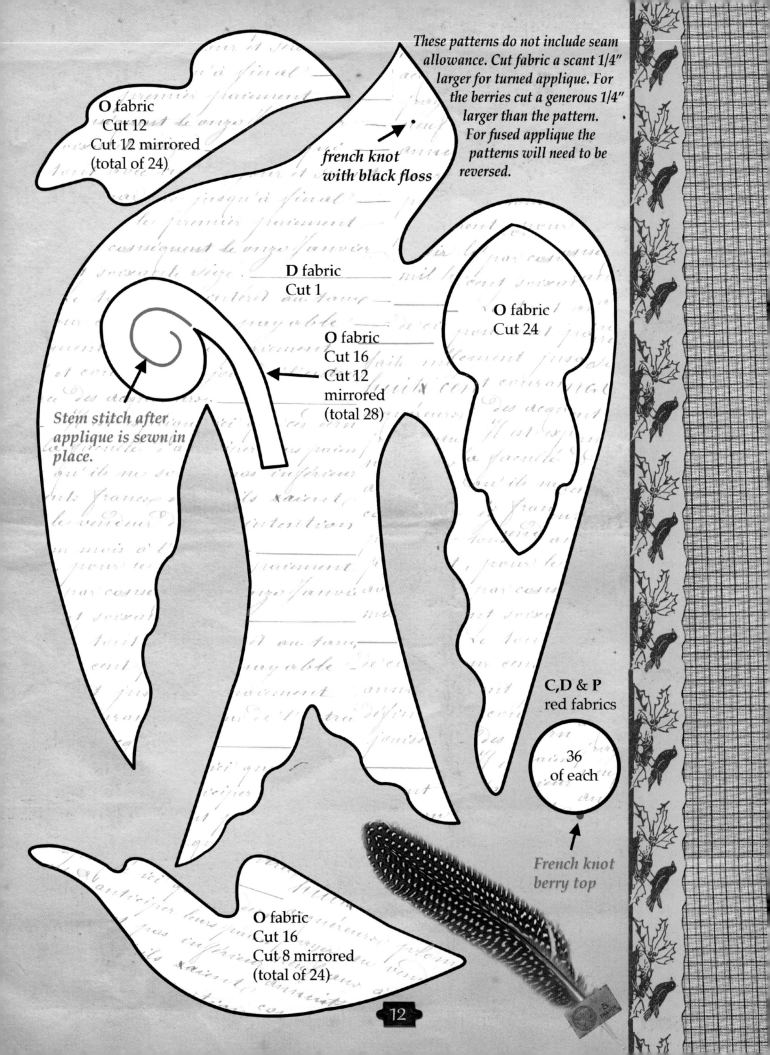

Embroidery Stitches

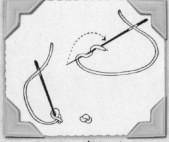

French Knot

Lazy Daisy

Chain Stitch

Running Stitch

Satin Stitch

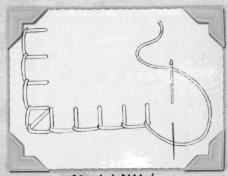

Blanket Stitch
(or Buttonhole Stitch)

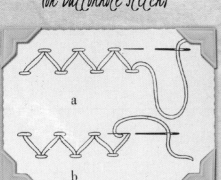

Back Stitch

Fly Stitch

Stroke Stitch

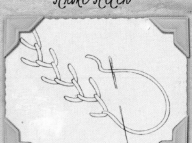

Feather Stitch

Chevron Stitch

Stem Stitch

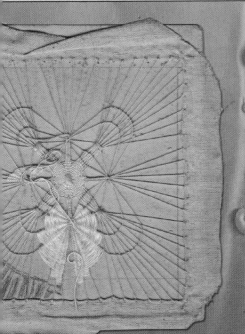

Jewelry Wrap

When traveling, a safe and pretty place to keep your favorite
jewelry pieces is a must. This jewelry keeper has three zippered
compartments for necklaces, bracelets, and earrings.
A padded ring holder keeps your rings safe and secure.

Jewelry Wrap

closed 4 1/2" x 7 1/2" - opened 7 1/2" x 16"
Jewelry Wrap design and monogrammed wrap by Bonnie Sullivan
Floral embroidery design by Kathy Schmitz
Jewelry on previous page created by Ann Fenderson / Next Chapter Jewelry

Supplies:

1/4 yard - Moda© 16" toweling -
Flag Day Farm Red
1/4 yard - Lining fabric
1/4 yard - Binding fabric
3 zippers 9" in length
1 button 3/4" - 1"
1 elastic hair band
1 large snap
small amount of stuffing
batting 8" x 16"
Floss -
Floral design embroidery -
  The Gentle Arts
    Simply Shaker - Pomegranate #7019
    Simply Shaker - Endive #7080
    Simply Shaker - Piney Woods #7082
    Simply Shaker - Toffee #7078
Monogram design cross stitch -
  The Gentle Arts
    Simply Shaker - Pomegranate #7019

Cutting:

Cut a 8" strip the width of the toweling fabric.
Cut a 8" strip the width of the lining fabric. Cut off the selvages.
Cut 2 strips 2 1/4" the width of the fabric for the binding.

Choose your design and use the guide below for placement.
Both designs should be centered on the toweling.

6 1/4"

7 3/4"

BS

toweling

toweling

Assembly:

Fold under 3 3/4" along one of the short ends of the lining fabric (A). Press well.
Open one of the zippers and pin to the folded edge as shown (B). Place the zipper so that the "teeth" of the zipper starts 3/8" below the lining
edge. Stitch 1/8" in from fabric fold. Unfold the fabric leaving this side of the zipper folded under (C).
Top stitch 1/4" from the fold (D).

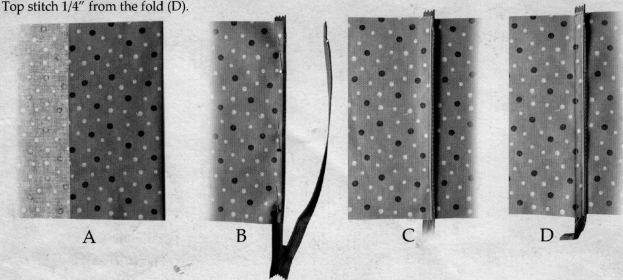

A   B   C   D

From the edge of the fabric fold measure 6 1/2" and fold the fabric again (E). Press well. Pin the other side of the zipper along this fold (F). Sew following steps B - D. Zip up the zipper.

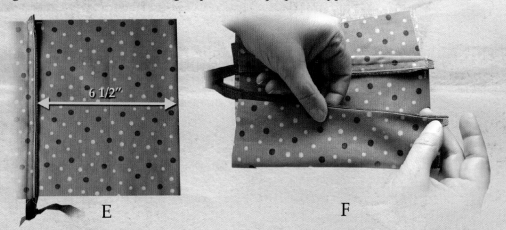

6 1/2"

E   F

Measure 3 3/4" down from the second fold and fold the fabric as in step A. Press well.
Sew on another zipper repeating steps B-D. Measure 6 1/2" down for the next fold. Press well. Sew on the other side of the zipper as in step F. Close the zipper. Measure 4 1/4" down, fold and sew on one side of the last zipper.
Measure 6 1/2" down for the final fold. Press well. Sew on the other side of the zipper following step F.

Cut off the end of the lining so that it is the same length as the toweling. From this extra fabric cut two pieces 2 1/2" x 4 3/4" for the ring tubes. Fold these pieces in half, right sides together, lengthwise, and sew the long sides together using a 1/4" seam. Rotate the tube so that the seam runs down the center of the back. Sew across one end of each of the tubes using a 1/4" seam. Turn the tubes right side out. Press. On the end that is sewn closed, sew a square with an X through it (see photo on the next page). Fill the tubes with stuffing up to 1/2" from the open ends.

Cut a piece of batting the same size as the lining and the toweling. Sandwich the toweling, batting and lining together. The toweling and the lining should have wrong sides facing each other. Pin all the way around. Pin the raw ends of the ring tubes in place as shown on the following page. Unzip the zipper about an inch so that the zipper head is out of the way. Using a scant 1/4" seam allowance sew all the way around, right over the extra zipper length. Cut off the excess zipper.

Sew two "compartments" in the last zippered section as shown on the following page.
Sew a snap over the "X" on the ring tubes to hold them together.

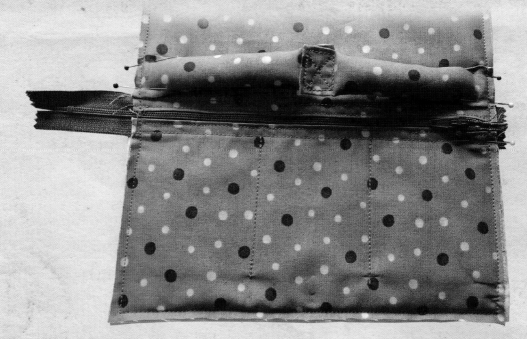

Sew on the binding following the binding directions on page 53.
Sew the binding to the toweling side of the jewelry keeper catching a small section of the elastic hair band at the center of the top edge. There should be about a 1" loop showing once the binding is finished. Once the binding is finished, fold up the jewelry keeper and sew the button so that the elastic loop will slip over it snuggly.

Use the images on page 19 to make the above pendants. The pendant blank information can be found on the resources page (see page 76).

Tiny trifles from years gone by are given new life when styled into wearable art. These necklaces were designed by Ann Fenderson; contact information can be found on page 76.

Embroider using 2 strands of embroidery floss. A Stitch guide may be found on page 13

A B C D E F
G H I J K L
M N O P Q
R S T U V W
X Y Z

Cross stitch using 2 strands of embroidery floss stitching over 1 thread.

All of the images on this page where found as we traveled the back roads of France

Hand painted clown from a dinner menu. The script is from an antique handwritten letter.

The cover of this antique compact seemed to be made for our paper weight project.

This is a page from an antique botany book found at the Lille flea market

Illustration from an antique book

To view finished paper weight projects see page 61
To view finished pendant projects see page 17

Toastie Toes

After an adventurous day discovering the twists & turns of ancient streets, it's nice to have a soft, warm pair of these woolen slippers to pamper your tired feet.

Toastie Toes

Floral slippers designed by Kathy Schmitz
Penny slippers designed by Bonnie Sullivan

Supplies: *Felt the wool (see page 53)*

Floral slippers -
    Black wool for slipper body - 1/2 yard (18" x 52")
    Wool scraps -Red, light green, medium green, & gold
    The Gentle Arts floss-
        Endive #7080, Tarnished Gold #0410 &
        Dark Chocolate #1170
    Red & Black 8 wt Perle cotton
    2 buttons 1/2" in diameter

Penny slippers
    Brown wool for slipper body 1/2 yard (18" x 52")
    Green wool for zigzag edge - 1" x 18"
    Assorted colors of wool - scraps
    8 wt Black Perle Cotton

A slow canoe ride down the Dordogne River was the perfect way to spend the afternoon & rest our tired tootsies.

Enlarge the slipper patterns according to the chart on page 23. Cut out 4 of the sole pieces and 4 of the slipper sides. Embroidery stitch guide is on page 13.

For the Floral slippers: trace the appliqué designs onto the paper side of freezer paper. Cut out pieces leaving a small amount around each piece. Iron pieces to the wool to be used. Cut out pieces and remove freezer paper. The freezer paper may be reused for the other slipper. Repeat this process for the other slipper (a total of 2 of everything). If you are using a wool that has a definite side to it, you will need to reverse the pattern pieces for the second slipper. Using the pattern as a guide, pin the vines in place and stitch using a matching thread and a whip stitch. Continue adding the other pieces from the background forward.

For the Penny slippers: cut out 3/4" circles in a variety of colors. Randomly place these circles on the sides of the slippers. Place them at least 1/2" away from all sides and within 2 1/4" from the bottom. We don't want these cute little pennies to be covered when the cuff is turned down. Using thread of a matching color, do a quick whip stitch around each circle to hold it in place. Using the Perle cotton, stitch fancy embroidery stitches around the circles. Use the Pennies to the right as a guide for your stitches.

Once all of the appliqué and embroidery is complete it's time to sew these tootsie warmers together. Using black 8 wt Perle cotton, buttonhole stitch the tops of the sides together. Now stitch the heal seam of the sides together. Right along the edge of the button hole stitches, back stitch from the top of the heal seam down 2". Repeat with the other slipper.

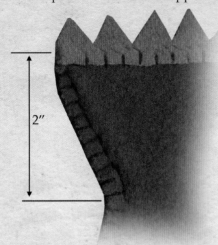

2"

For the Penny slippers, now is the time to sew on the green zigzag edging. Starting at the center seam (top of the arch not the heal), slip stitch the green wool to the brown on the Penny side of the slipper using a brown thread.

On the other side of the slipper, buttonhole stitch around the opening. This edge will flip over to form the cuff.

For the floral slippers, buttonhole stitch around the opening using the Endive floss. Sew the buttons onto the the cuff, at the curve, to hold the folded cuff in place.

For both the Floral and the Penny slippers, machine stitch the 2 soul pieces together using a 1/4" seam and matching thread. Repeat with the other 2 soul pieces. Pin the tops to the souls, wrong sides together. Start by pinning the center of the heals and the tips of the toes then continue pinning around the entire soul. Buttonhole stitch around the entire bottom of the slippers (red Perle cotton for the Floral slippers and black Perle cotton for the Penny slippers).

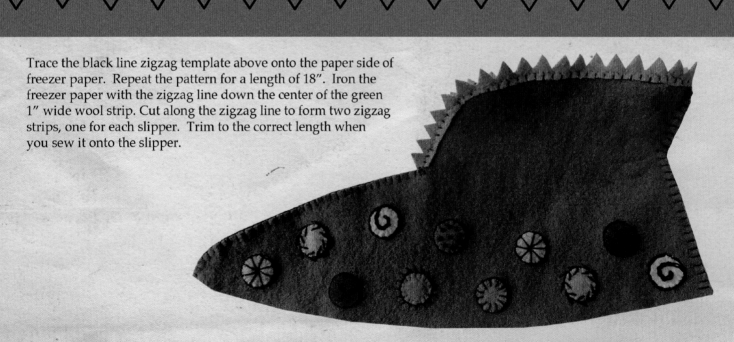

Trace the black line zigzag template above onto the paper side of freezer paper. Repeat the pattern for a length of 18". Iron the freezer paper with the zigzag line down the center of the green 1" wide wool strip. Cut along the zigzag line to form two zigzag strips, one for each slipper. Trim to the correct length when you sew it onto the slipper.

If you want to relive your childhood days of sliding across the hardwood floors in your hand knitted slippers, these are guaranteed to give you a good slide. We have found however, that the older we become the more it hurts when we take a tumble. It is a good idea to sew some sort of anti-skid surface to the bottoms of these beauties.

side - cut 2

When tracing these appliqué patterns onto the paper, extend any pieces that will be placed behind another piece.

All of the embroidery stitches on the floral appliqué are done using 2 strands of floss. Leaf veins are stitched in Endive using a fly stitch. The stitches on the berries are stroke stitches in Tarnished Gold. The stitches on the green circles are stroke stitches done in the Tarnished Gold. The embroidery accents are chain stitches, fly stitches and French knots in Tarnished Gold. The cross hatched centers are stitched using the Dark Chocolate.

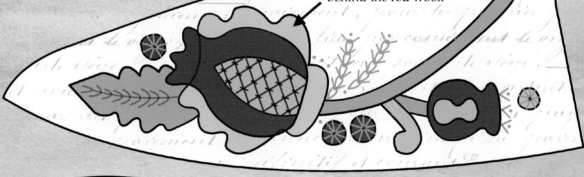

side - cut 2

This green piece may be cut as one piece and placed behind the red wool.

sole - cut 4

Photocopy and enlarge the above patterns according to the chart below or so that the sole pattern is 1/2" longer than your foot. Adjust accordingly. These slippers are wide, loose and comfy. They are not intended to be snug.

Small - 6 - 7 1/2 increase 191%
Medium - 8 -10 increase 202%
Large - 10 1/2 - 12 increase 214%

She would have loved slippers like these!

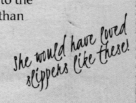

Shoe Sachet & Cozy

These lavender sachets will add a lovely scent to your shoes.
Slip them into your shoes, then store them in their very own cozy!

Shoe Cozy & Sachet

draw string cozy 11" x 14 1/2"

Appliqué draw string Shoe Cozy & Sachets designed by Kathy Schmitz
Monogrammed draw string Shoe Cozy designed by Bonnie Sullivan

Supplies:

For the appliqué Shoe Cozy draw string bag
you will need:
Green print for the body of the bag - 5/8 yard
Light plaid for the appliqué background - 8" x 8"
Fabric scraps in dark green, light green, three shades of red,
    brown, & goldish brown.
Floss - The Gentle Arts
    Sampler Threads - Dark Chocolate #1170
    Simply Shaker - Piney Woods #7082
    Simply Shaker - Pomegranate #7019
1" wide grosgrain ribbon - 1 yard
Two sided fusible web - 5" x 8 1/2"

For the Monogrammed Shoe Cozy draw string bag
you will need:
Floral print for the body of the bag - 5/8 yard
Red print for the center trim - 2 pieces 1" x 6 1/2"
    2 pieces 1" x 7 1/2"
Antique linen, embroidered piece, or other nice fabric
to use as the focal center piece - 6 1/2"x 6 1/2"
  *The center piece in this sample (see below) Bonnie found
at a flea market in Lille. When she saw the cross-stitched
"B" she knew she had to have it.*
1" wide grosgrain ribbon - 1 yard

For the Shoe Sachets you will need -
Light fabric - 1/4 yard
Red print - 1/8 yard
Two sided fusible web - 8 1/2" x 11"
Lavender and batting

*Antique linens can be found at every
flea market. Find one that is
special to you and make your
shoe cozy unique.*

Appliqué:

Trace the appliqué patterns onto the two sided fusible web following the manufacturers directions.
Cut the pieces out leaving extra around each piece (do not cut them out on the traced line). Remove the paper backing from the fusible web. Stick the fusible web pieces to the wrong side of the corresponding fabric to be used. Iron according to the fusible web directions. Cut out the pieces along the traced lines. Following the guide, beginning with the background pieces first, arrange the appliqué pieces onto the center of the appliqué background piece of fabric. Iron the pieces in place. These may be stitched around to secure the edges if you choose. Trim the applique background fabric to 7 1/2" x 7 1/2" with the design centered.

Cutting:

Draw string bag (both appliqué and monogrammed)
From the body fabric, cut 1 strip 12 1/2" wide by width of fabric.. Trim off the selvage and trim to 42" in length.
From the body fabric, cut 1 strip 7 1/2" wide by the width of the fabric. From this piece cut 2 pieces 3" by 7 1/2" and 2 pieces 6" x 12 1/2".

Assembly: 1/4" seam allowance unless otherwise noted

Monogram bag: Sew the two 1" x 6 1/2" red strips to the sides of the monogrammed center square. Press.
    Sew the two 1" x 7 1/2" red strips to the top and bottom of the center piece. Press.
For both the appliqué bag and the monogrammed bag:
Sew one of the body pieces 3" x 7 1/2" to one side of the center piece. Press
Sew the other 3" x 7 1/2" piece to the other side. Press.
Sew one of the 6" x 12 1/2" pieces to the *top* of the center piece. Press.
Sew the other 6" x 12 1/2" piece to the 12 1/2" x 42" long piece. Press.
Sew the bottom of the appliqué/monogrammed center section to the end of the 42" long piece without the 6" addition.
Press Now you will have one very long piece (A).
With the right sides together sew the short sides together using a 5/8" seam. Press the seam open.
Fold the loop so that the 5/8" seam is at the top. Finger press across the bottom of the loop.

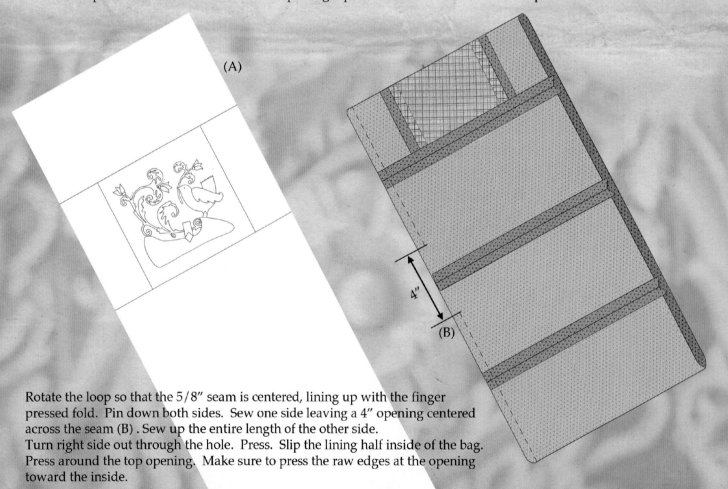

(A)

(B)

4"

Rotate the loop so that the 5/8" seam is centered, lining up with the finger pressed fold. Pin down both sides. Sew one side leaving a 4" opening centered across the seam (B) . Sew up the entire length of the other side.
Turn right side out through the hole. Press. Slip the lining half inside of the bag.
Press around the top opening. Make sure to press the raw edges at the opening toward the inside.

Stitch around the top of the bag opening 2" down from the edge . Sew around the top again, 1" down from the top edge, forming a 1" casing.

Thread the ribbon through the casing. Tie the two ends of the ribbon together. Pull the ribbon to gather and close the shoe cozy. It might be a good idea to place a plastic bag inside of this pretty cozy just in case your shoes have been traipsing through the woods.

Shoe Sachet Assembly: 1/4" seam allowance

Trace the entire sachet pattern side (A) and the shoe "sole" pattern (B) onto a piece of paper and cut them out.

Trace the "shoe" pattern (C) onto the double stick fusible web following the manufacturer's directions.

You will need a total of four "shoes" (C) traced onto the fusible web, *two in each direction*. Do not cut them out yet.

Stick the fusible web "shoes" onto the back side of the red fabric. Follow the fusible web manufacturer's directions.

Cut out the "shoes" in the red fabric.

Cut the selvages off the Light Fabric. Cut this strip into four sections, each at least 10" long.

Stick the red fabric with the fusible web to each of the light fabric pieces as shown.

Following the manufacturer's directions iron them in place. There will be two in each direction.

Place the side paper pattern (A) on top of the "shoe" and light fabric, lining up the bottom, heel and toe, and trace around the pattern. This will be your cutting line. Repeat with the other three pieces. Cut out these four sides with the fused "shoes". Using the "sole" (B) paper pattern cut out 2 "soles" from the red fabric.

With the right sides together, sew the left and right sides of the foot together leaving the entire bottom open. Clip and press the seams. Finger press the "sole" in half lengthwise at the toe and heel. Match up the heel finger press to the heel seam of the sides, right sides together, and pin. Match up the toe the same way and pin. Pin around the rest of the "sole". Machine sew around the bottom leaving a 3" opening along one of the straight sides. Clip and trim the seam as needed. Turn right side out. Press the raw edges of the opening toward the inside 1/4". Repeat with the other shoe sachet. Fill the sachets with a mixture of lavender and batting. Hand stitch the openings closed.

Appliqué pattern

Embroidery for
appliqué image:
(2 strands of floss)
Bird legs - stem stitch in
Dark Chocolate Brown.
Bird tail and eye
dots - French
knots in
Dark
Chocolate
Brown.
Dots by
leaves -
French knots in
Pomegranate.

The doors of Notre Dame Cathedral were the
inspiration for the appliqué design. Kathy loved
the swirls of the leaves and tendrils.

These fun shoes, purchased
from a street vendor in
Lille, were the inspiration
for the colorful "shoes"
on the sachets.

C
shoes

A
sides

B
soles

my memories

Mes
Souvenirs

Mes Souvenirs (My Memories)

Embroidered Journal Cover designed by Kathy Schmitz
Antique Tapestry Journal Cover designed by Bonnie Sullivan

Supplies:

Embroidered Cover:
Moda© 16" toweling Red Day Farm - 1 yard
Spine fabric - 6" x 10 1/2"
1" button with a shank & 1/2" button with 4 holes
Embroidery floss - The Gentle Arts
   Simply Shaker - Pomegranate #7019
   Simply Shaker - Mountain Mist #7045
   Simply Shaker - Endive #7080
Elastic hair band

Antique Tapestry Cover:
A piece of needlepoint measuring 10 5/8" x 16 1/2"
Lining & spine fabric - 1/4 yard
1" button
Elastic Hair Band

A sketch or two and notes to remember the trip by are treasures to look back on. These two pages document our day in Brugge, Belgium spent with our new friends Raymond (travel guide extraordinaire), and his lovely daughter Christel.

Embroidered Journal Cover: Use 2 strands of floss.
Zigzag stitch the two cut ends of the toweling to keep it from raveling.
Trace the embroidery design onto the toweling following the diagram for placement. The bird and banner outline are stitched in Pomegranate using a stem stitch. The stems and leaves are stitched in Endive. Use a stem stitch for the stems and Lazy Daisy for the leaves. The berries and bird's eye are stitched in Pomegranate using French knots. The lettering is stitched in Pomegranate using a chain stitch with a Mountain Mist stem stitch along the left side. See detail of letter stitches on the next page.

Once all of the embroidery is complete, trim the toweling to 10 1/2" wide, with the stripes centered. From the end of the toweling with the embroidery measure 31" and cut away excess toweling. Finished size is 10 1/2" x 31" Zigzag the raw edges.

This is sized to fit a standard composition book. If you want to use a book with different dimensions you will need to adjust the measurements accordingly.
*Example: Measure the book, closed, from the edge of the front cover to the edge of the back cover, over the spine. Double that measurement and subtract 1". This will be your **length**.*
*Measure the height of the book + 3/4". This will be your **width**.*
It is always a good idea to make up a dummy cover out of a similar weight fabric first.

toweling

9 1/4"

Assemble:

For the embroidery cover

Fold the shorter ends of the toweling under 1/2", press and top stitch 1/4" from the edge using a matching thread. Turn the shorter ends in (right sides together) 7 1/8" toward the center. This should leave about 1 1/4" - 1 1/2" in between where the two edges come together. Pin in place.

Place the spine piece, right side down, over the center and pin it in place. Using a 1/4" seam, sew across the top and bottom of the cover. Trim the corners and turn it right side out. Sew the 1" button to the front of the cover with the button edge about 1/4" in from the edge of the journal cover and about 3" down from the top. On the back side, sew on the 1/2" button about 1" in from the edge and 3" down from the top. When sewing on the 1/2" button slip the elastic hair band between it and the cover and secure the band in place. Be careful not to sew through to the lining. Slip the composition book inside the journal cover. The elastic band will wrap around the button on the cover to hold your journal closed.

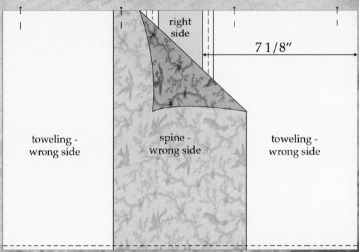

letter embroidery detail

For the Antique Tapestry cover

This cover was sewn using an antique needlepoint piece. Because this fabric is so heavy we have added a little bit more to the measurements (1/8" - 1/4"). If you are using a heavy fabric, this might be a good idea for you also.

Cut the lining and spine fabric into 2 pieces 7 1/4" x 10 5/8"(lining) and 1 piece 6" x 10 5/8" (spine). *Side note: if your your lining fabric is thin, iron interfacing to the backside to give it stability.* On the 7 1/4" x 10 5/8" lining pieces fold under 1/2" on one of the 10 5/8" sides press and top stitch 1/4" from the edge. Lay the trimmed tapestry (10 5/8" x 16 1/2") face up. Place a lining piece on each end, right sides together, with the turned under edge toward the middle.

Place the 6" x 10 5/8" spine piece over the center (see above diagram). Sew according to the directions above with one exception: Sew the elastic hair band in the seam at the back of the book, centered between the top and the bottom of the cover. Sew the button to the front of the cover so that it lines up with the elastic band placement.

Pocket Locket

Nest Scarf

to market
to market

Market Bag

Photography by Sean Sullivan / Model Erynn Gerber

Pocket Locket 3 1/2" x 4 3/4"

designed by Bonnie Sullivan

Supplies: *Felt the wool (see page 53)*
Brown wool for the body of the purse - 4" x 11 1/2"
Lining fabric - 4" x 11 1/2"
Two sided fusible web - 4" x 11 1/2"
Wool scraps - light and dark rusty red, gold and green
Perle cotton 5 wt - green, rusty orange, gold, brown & black.
1 black snap - 1/2"
36" long brown shoelace with finished ends

Appliqué:
Trace the appliqué patterns onto the dull side of freezer paper. Cut them out leaving extra around each piece. Iron the wax side to the wool. Cut out the pieces on the traced lines. Remove the freezer paper. Using the diagram on the following page, arrange the appliqué pieces and whip stitch them in place using a coordinating color of thread.

This little pouch is just big enough to hold your hotel key & Euros when you want to travel light.

Once the wool pieces have been sewn in place, it's time to add the embroidery embellishments. Using the green Perle cotton and a stem stitch, stitch the vines for the leaves. Reference the image to the left for embroidery details. The gold dots are French knots, the fly stitches are done in rusty orange and the buttonhole stitch and the center French knot are done in black. Sandwich the fusible web between the wrong sides of the lining and the wool. Fuse the layers together by ironing on the *lining* side following the manufacturer's directions. Let it cool completely. Using the pattern template on the next page, cut out the pocket body with the design centered. Using the brown Perle cotton, buttonhole stitch across the straight end. Fold this end up along the dotted line and blanket stitch around the remaining raw edges. Along the dotted line, near the curved end, whip stitch the center of the shoelace without going through to the wool. Sew on the snap as shown above. Tie the ends of the shoelaces together.

Keep your hands free to carry flowers from the market. Bring your money & hotel key in a sweet little Pocket Locket

Trace the outline of the pocket pattern onto a piece freezer paper and cut it out. Iron the wax side of the freezer paper to the finished applique piece with the design centered. Cut out the pocket piece.

start the buttonhole stitch here ▶ with a long length of Perle cotton to assure there are no knots on this curved flap.

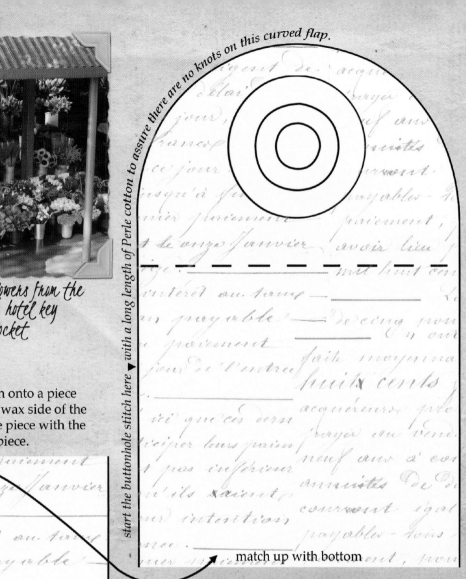

match up to top

match up with bottom

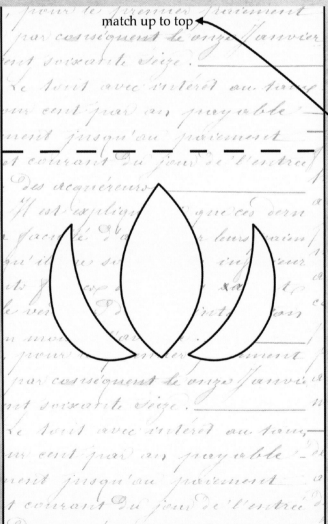

1/2"

11 1/2"

2"

4"

...and don't forget the fresh baguette!

Nest Scarf

designed by Kathy Schmitz

Approximately 7" x 60"
Adjust the length as needed by piecing more wool for the body of the scarf.

Supplies: *felt the wool (see page 53)*
Wool for the body of the scarf - 7" x width of wool - at least 52"
Dark Blue zigzag border wool - 2 pieces 8" x 5"
Army Green appliqué background wool - 4 pieces 4" x 7 1/4" (A & B)
Vine wool - 4 pieces 1/4" x 7 1/4 & 8 pieces 1/4" x 1"
Leaf wool - 6" x 8"
Scraps of wool in berry red, bird blue, autumn tweed & egg blue
Floss - The Gentle Arts
   Endive #7080, Soot #1050, Crystal Lake #7075, Pomegranate #7019
4 black snaps 1/2"

*Secret pockets in the back
are just the right size
for a few Euros and a hotel key.*

Assembly:

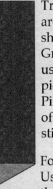

Trace the pattern pieces onto the paper side of freezer paper. Cut them apart leaving extra around the patterns. Iron the freezer paper to the wool colors to be used. Cut out the shapes and peel off the freezer paper. Pin a piece of the 7 1/4" long vine wool to the Army Green appliqué wool (A) following the diagrams on the next page. Whip stitch it in place using a thread of similar color. Repeat with all 4 of the pieces. On two of these Army Green pieces (A), pin the short vine pieces in place following the diagrams. Whip stitch in place. Pin on the remaining pieces, background to foreground and whip stitch in place. Once all of the pieces are stitched down, embroider the details following the diagrams for color and stitches. Embroider using 2 strands of floss. *Embroidery stitch guide is found on page 13.*

Fold the Dark Blue zigzag wool piece over the ends of the scarf body on the fold line. Using a matching thread color and shallow stitches, so that they don't show, whip stitch the zigzag edges onto both sides of the scarf. Whip stitch the sides closed.

On the two pieces (B) without the bird and the nest, fold under the top 1/2" and top stitch 1/4" from the top. Place the bird section (A) on top of the zigzag wool at one end of the scarf over-lapping 1" of the folded end. Flip the scarf over and place one of the appliqué sections (B) on top of the bird section matching up the bottom and the sides. The top stitched side will go UNDER the zigzagged fold. These should overlap about 1/2", just enough for two snaps. Buttonhole around the sides and the bottom and across the top of the bird (A) section using 2 strands of the soot floss. Buttonhole around them again using the Endive floss, placing the stitches between each other. Repeat these steps on the other end using the nest section and the other (A) section with the (A) sections on the same side of the scarf.

Sew on the snaps. Go shopping!

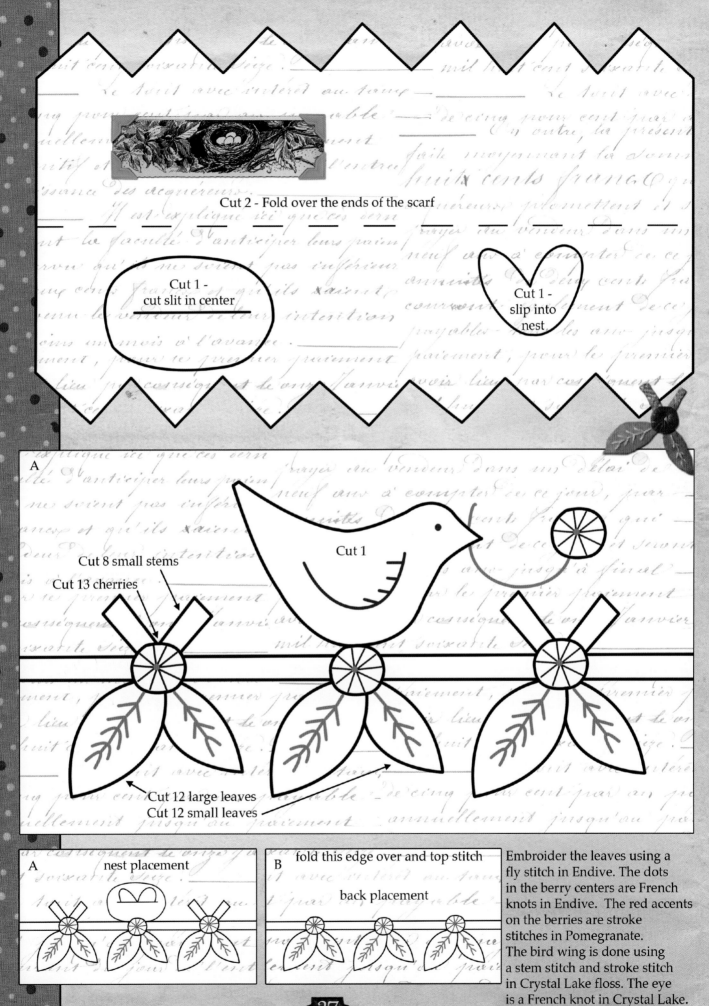

Cut 2 - Fold over the ends of the scarf

Cut 1 -
cut slit in center

Cut 1 -
slip into
nest

A

Cut 8 small stems

Cut 13 cherries

Cut 1

Cut 12 large leaves
Cut 12 small leaves

A   nest placement

B   fold this edge over and top stitch

back placement

Embroider the leaves using a
fly stitch in Endive. The dots
in the berry centers are French
knots in Endive. The red accents
on the berries are stroke
stitches in Pomegranate.
The bird wing is done using
a stem stitch and stroke stitch
in Crystal Lake floss. The eye
is a French knot in Crystal Lake.

Market Bag *approximately 13" x 13"*

Bag design by Bonnie Sullivan & Kathy Schmitz

Applique design by Bonnie Sullivan

Supplies: *felt the wool (see page 53)*
Heavy weight woven brown fabric for the body,
handle & lining - 1 1/2 yards
Inside pocket fabric - 1/4 yard
Black wool - 8" x 12"
Green wool - 5" x 6"
2 red wools - 2" x 2"
1 red wool 2" x 2" & 2 strips - 3/4" x 12"
   for the ruching
3 - 1 1/4" covered button blanks
Brown 8 wt Perle cotton to match the brown fabric.

Cutting:
Heavy brown fabric:
   Cut 4 - 5" strips across width of fabric for the
purse gusset/straps. The width of the fabric
should be at least 42".
   Cut 1 pleated purse front.
   Cut 1 purse back and 2 purse linings.
   Cut 1 - 5 1/2" x 16" piece for the
shoulder section.
Inside pocket fabric:
   Cut 2 - 8" x 20" pieces
Black wool:
   Cut 1 yoke piece.
Green wool:
   Cut 3 leaves

We love market day!

mmmm...

Many towns have market day
once a week. It's a great
place to pick up fresh bread,
fruit and salami for lunch.
FYI-Autruche means Ostrich

The dashed line is the center fold. Flip this side over on the dashed line to complete the yoke pattern.

cut 1 yoke
black wool

Assembly:

Arrange wool leaves on the yoke of the purse using the diagram below as a guide and whip stitch in place using green thread. Using brown Perle cotton and a stem stitch, stitch the branch and veins of the leaves. Cover the 3 - 1 1/4" button blanks with the 3 different colors of red wool (2" x 2" square) following the directions that came with the button blanks.

Fold the pleat in on both sides of the pleated purse front matching up the red dots, and run a line of stitching along the slanted upper edges of the purse pivoting at the center dot 1/2" in from the edge.

Cut 1 yoke

fold here to make the pattern for the yoke

Lay the completed black wool yoke onto the pleated purse front so the sides match up and so the bottom edge of the yoke extends 1/8" beyond the line of stitching on the pleated purse front.

The back side of the yoke will overlap onto the right side of the pleated purse front. Sew the yoke onto the pleated purse front 1/8" up from the bottom of the yoke which should be directly on top of the line of stitching on the pleated purse front. (*Sorry for the run-on sentences*)

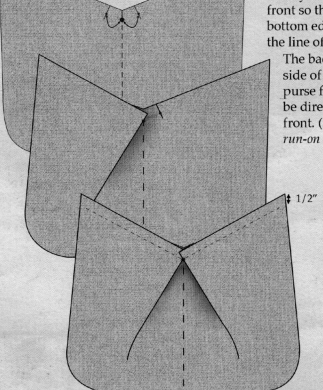

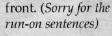
1/2"

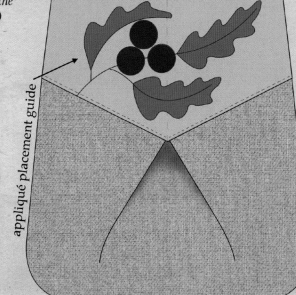
appliqué placement guide

The dashed line is the center fold. Flip this side over on the dashed line to complete the pleated front pattern.

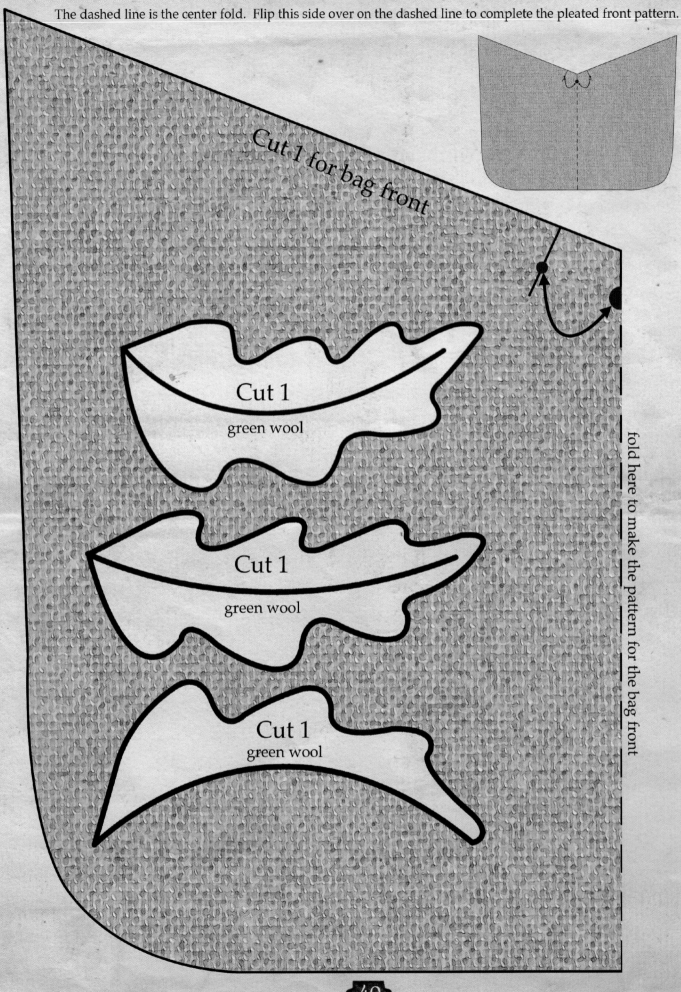

Cut 1 for bag front

Cut 1

green wool

Cut 1

green wool

Cut 1

green wool

fold here to make the pattern for the bag front

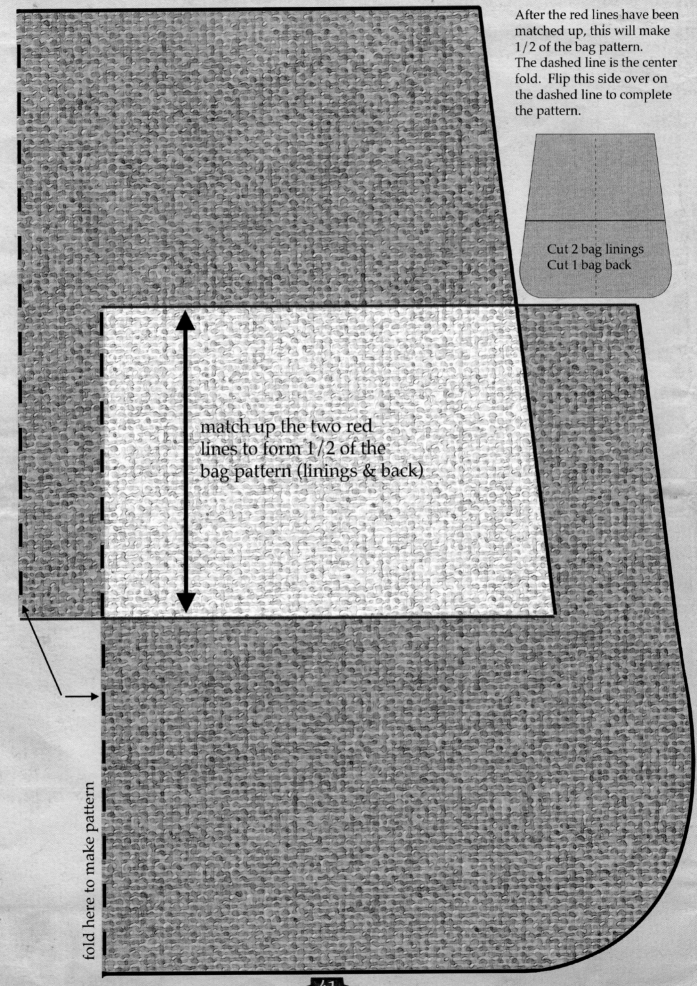

After the red lines have been matched up, this will make 1/2 of the bag pattern. The dashed line is the center fold. Flip this side over on the dashed line to complete the pattern.

Cut 2 bag linings
Cut 1 bag back

match up the two red lines to form 1/2 of the bag pattern (linings & back)

fold here to make pattern

Use the 2 - 3/4" x 12" strips of red wool to make the ruching (a French term that means gathering, ruffling or pleating). Run a gathering stitch down the center of the red strips. Gather each strip to fit one half of the bottom edge of the black wool yoke. Make sure there are NO gathers 1/2" in on one of the ends of each strip. Sew a line of stitching over the gathers to hold them in place. Remove the basting thread if it shows. Stitch ruched strips to the bottom edge of the yoke, directly over the line of stitching that stitched the yoke to the pleated purse front. Make sure the ends of the two strips which are not gathered, are lined up with the outside edges of the purse front and the gathered ends meet at the center of the yoke.

Fold 8" x 20" pocket fabric in half.

Stitch with 1/2 seam allowance down the sides.

Turn right side out and press. Topstitch 1/4" in from fold.

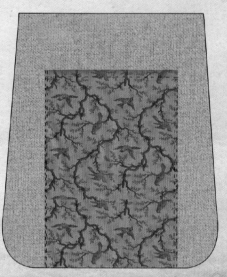

Line up raw edges of the pocket with the bottom of the back lining. Stitch using a 1/4" topstitch and another topstitch right along the edge of the pocket. Repeat these steps for the other lining.

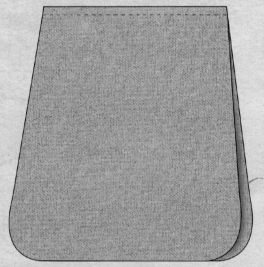

Across the top of the bag, stitch a lining to the back piece, right sides together, using a 1/2" seam. Repeat this step with the purse front and lining.

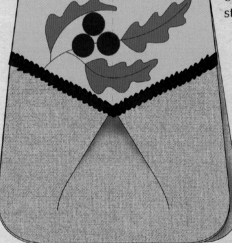

Flip both of these pieces right side out and press. Topstitch across the tops 1/4" in.

original idea sketch

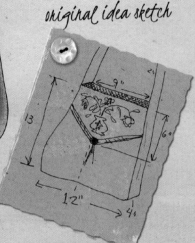

If you have used a loosely woven fabric for the bag, to prevent raveling, zigzag the two layers of the purse front and backs to their linings.

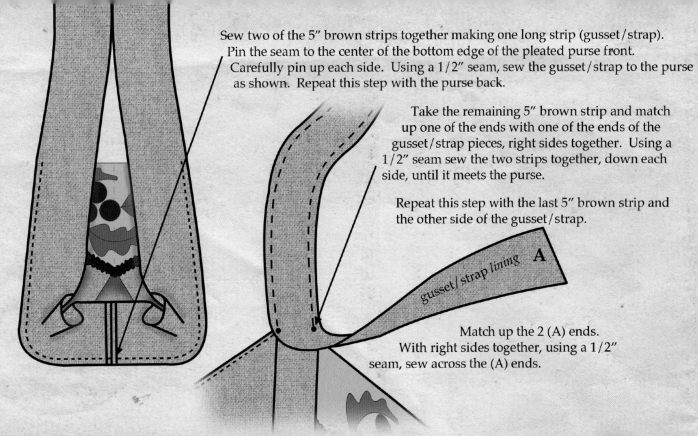

Sew two of the 5" brown strips together making one long strip (gusset/strap). Pin the seam to the center of the bottom edge of the pleated purse front. Carefully pin up each side. Using a 1/2" seam, sew the gusset/strap to the purse as shown. Repeat this step with the purse back.

Take the remaining 5" brown strip and match up one of the ends with one of the ends of the gusset/strap pieces, right sides together. Using a 1/2" seam sew the two strips together, down each side, until it meets the purse.

Repeat this step with the last 5" brown strip and the other side of the gusset/strap.

gusset/strap lining A

Match up the 2 (A) ends. With right sides together, using a 1/2" seam, sew across the (A) ends.

Pin the (A) seam to the center of the bottom edge of the pleated purse front. Carefully pin up each side. Using a 1/2" seam, sew the gusset/strap *lining* pieces as you did with the gusset/strap at the top of this page. Follow the same line of stitching.

Turn the straps right side out. On the remaining raw side of the gusset/strap *lining*, press under 1/2". Place that pressed, folded edge over the gusset/strap & purse seam with all raw edges facing toward the gusset/strap. Using a whip stitch, sew the gusset/strap *lining* in place. Your market bag will have no raw edges!

Determine how long you would like your strap to be by overlapping the two unfinished ends. While they are overlapped, cut an even amount off of both ends.

Take the 5 1/2" x 16" piece of brown fabric and fold in half lengthwise with right sides together. Using a 1/2" seam, sew the two long edges together. Press the seam open. Turn right side out.
Turn the raw edges back inside of the tube until they meet. The finished piece will be 8" long (doubled thickness).
Slid the tube over one of the straps about 1/2 way exposing at least 6" of the gusset/strap. This was Bonnie's idea, blame her.

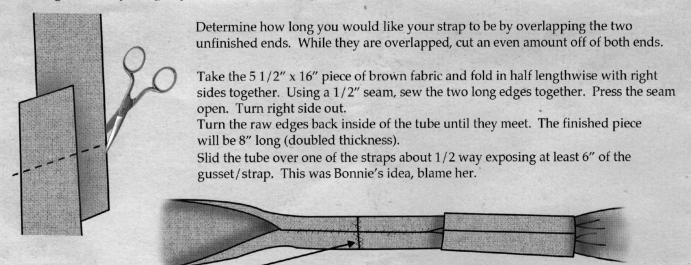

Whip stitch the raw ends of the gusset/strap together, abutting the ends, making sure the strap is not twisted.

Fold the two sides of the gusset/strap toward the middle of the strap, about 3"- 4" on either side of the center whip stitched seam. Whip stitch those edges together as shown in the above diagram.

Using a denim needle, and a strong thread, stitch across both ends of the tube through gusset/strap. MANY layers! *If this was a cake it would be delicious!*

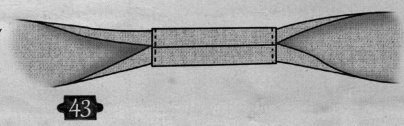

...re Les époux Meuou, acquérereu...

...claré que l'acquisition qu'ils vena...

...e est pour Madame Souton, é...

..., qui l'a acceptée comme devant

...vir de remploi anticipé de s...

...nbles dotaux qu'elle a l'intentio...

...re incessamment, avec l'autorisa...

...mari, remploi auquel elle est

... par son contrat de mariage

...devant Maître Dumontpallu...

...e à Ahun, le six Janvier m...

...ent soixante Sept, aux termes

...e ils ont adopté le régime dot...

...mmunauté d'acquêts.. Devant M...

...aître Lors du paiement de la pres...

...ition aux époques qui ont été

...fixées, Monsieur et Madame R...

...connaître l'origine des denier...

Framed Collage

The antique script on the opposite page is a perfect backdrop to show off treasures collected along the way. The script page was found at a flea market in Paris. The aged paper and imperfect pen and ink writing makes it a unique background layer.

Create your own collages using some of the images on the inspiration pages found throughout the book.

Laser copy the script page (inkjet ink may smear when glued). Permission is given to copy page 44 for personal use.

Amour de la couture
Love of sewing

Marqueyssac
Doves

Symbole de paix
Symbol of peace

Marqueyssac Doves
10" long x 6" high

Dove pattern designed by Bonnie Sullivan

Peace Dove designed by Bonnie Sullivan

Tomato Dove designed by Kathy Schmitz

Supplies: *felt the wool (see page 53)*
For the Peace Dove your will need:
Cream Wool 12" x 24"
Perle cotton 5 wt - color to match wool
1/2" wide ribbon for neck - 6" length
2 - 3/4" ivory buttons
Stuffing

For the Tomato Dove you will need:
Tomato red wool 12" x 24"
Green accent wool -scrap
Floss - The Gentle Arts Simply Shaker Piney Woods #7082
2 - 3/4" black buttons
An old thimble
Stuffing

Cutting:
Trace the pattern on the next page onto the paper side of freezer paper. You will need 4 wings (2 in each direction), 2 sides (1 in each direction), and 1 bird bottom. Mark the dots on the sides and bottom. Cut them out leaving extra around the drawn line. Iron the wax side onto the wool placing the arrows along the straight of grain. Cut out the pieces on the drawn lines.
For the Tomato Dove you will also need the green pattern pieces cut. For the green collar start with a piece of wool 3/4" x 5". Loosely cut zigzags along one side. For the top knot and the thimble fill, cut 2 circles of wool 1 1/2" in diameter each. From one cut zigzags around the edge. The other one will cover the stuffing inside of the thimble. This may need to be trimmed to fit your thimble.

Embroidery: **Peace Dove**
Using the embroidery design guide on the next page, and the Perle cotton, embroider the wing designs on the two wings - one in each direction.

Sewing:
With the right sides together, using a 1/4" seam, sew the wings together. Sew all the way around. Cut a slit on the backside of the wings for turning. Turn and press. Whip stitch the slit closed. With the right sides together, match up the dots on the bird's sides and bottom. Pin. Sew using a 1/4" seam, stopping and starting at the dots, sew both sides of the bird to the bottom. Sew the top of the bird together leaving a small opening on it's back. Flatten the tail so the seam sewing the two bird halves together is centered. Sew across the tail. Trim and clip where needed. Turn the bird right side out. Stuff and hand stitch the opening closed.

Nestled in the hills of the Perigord are the Gardens of Marqueyssac. Filled with thousands of perfectly manicured boxwoods, overlooking the Dordogne River, we spent an afternoon strolling the 22 acres. On the tip top of one of the buildings we spotted this sweet dove. She was the inspiration for our Marqueyssac Dove.

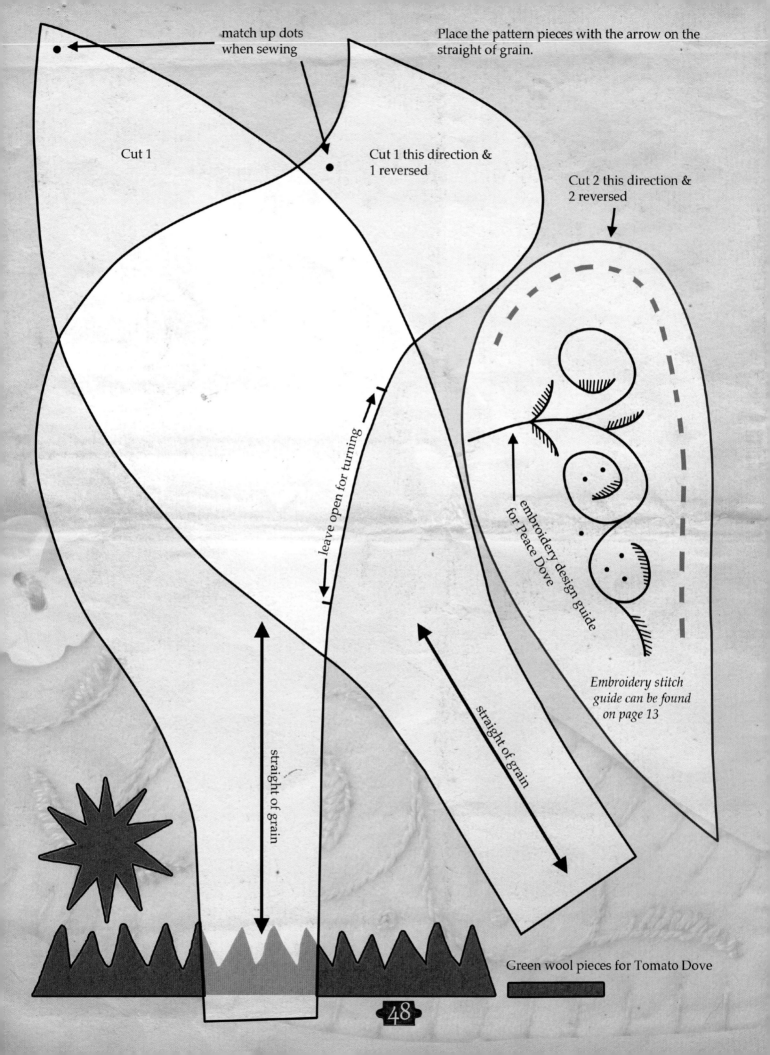

match up dots
when sewing

Place the pattern pieces with the arrow on the straight of grain.

Cut 1

Cut 1 this direction &
1 reversed

Cut 2 this direction &
2 reversed

leave open for turning

embroidery design guide
for Peace Dove

*Embroidery stitch
guide can be found
on page 13*

straight of grain

straight of grain

Green wool pieces for Tomato Dove

On the seams of the bird, from the neck down and along the bottom, fly stitch over the seams. Embroidery stitches may be found on page 13. For the Peace Dove use the Perle cotton. For the Tomato Dove use 2 strands of the green floss. Using the same threads, sew buttonhole stitches around the wings. Make French knots for the eyes pulling the needle all the way through the head so that the eyes are slightly indented. Following the rust colored dashed line on the wing pattern, hand stitch the wings to the bird. Sew the buttons in place.

For the Peace Dove attach the ribbon around the neck with the seam under the neck. Sew a small stem of boxwood to the beak.

For the Tomato Dove attach the green zigzag strip around the neck using French knots, with the seam under the neck. Sew the round zigzag piece to the top of the head using French knots. At the very top of this, add the tiny strip folded in half with the folded end on the bird head. Sew the top loose ends of this strip together with a tiny stitch.

To attach the thimble, drill two tiny holes across from each other on the thimble. Place a small amount of stuffing inside of the thimble. Cover the stuffing with the green wool circle, tucking the edges inside of the thimble. With heavy red thread attach the thimble to the bird's beak threading it through the drilled holes. To add a fun touch place a needle in the thimble stuffing. Dip a doubled up strand of the red thread into fabric stiffener or watered down white glue and let it dry on a piece of wax paper, shape as desired. Once it is dry thread it through the needle.

To display these Doves find a large wooden finial or turned candle holder. Drill a tiny hole down the center. Insert a small firm wire so that 2" or so sticks out of the top. Pierce the Dove onto the wire. We know this sounds brutal, but it looks great!

A "birds" eye view from the gardens

Brantôme

Brantôme 64" x 80"

Designed by Bonnie Sullivan
Pieced by Margie Bergan
Quilted by Pam Parvin/Quilting

Supplies & Cutting:

Four light print fabrics - 3/4 yard each
From each light fabric cut as follows:
Cut 2 - 5" strips across the width of the fabric. Cut 5" strips
   into 20 - 5" squares. Draw a diagonal line on the back of
   each 5" square.
Cut 5 - 2 1/2" strips across the width of the fabric.

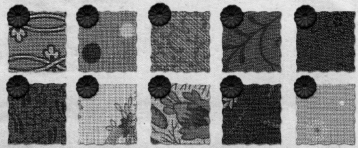

The Abbey of Brantôme had a magnificent staircase. The pattern looking down the stairs was the inspiration for this pieced quilt. Brantôme was a darling city which sits on the river Dronne. It also had one of the best brocante (antique) shops!

10 different medium to dark fabrics - 3/8 yard each
From each medium to dark fabric:
Cut 1 - 5" strip across with of fabric. Cut 5" strips into 8 - 5" squares.
Cut 2 - 2 1/2" strips across width of fabric.

Assembly: all seam allowances are 1/4"

1. Each of the 20 blocks in this quilt is made up of a combination of one of the light fabrics and one of the medium to dark fabrics. Randomly pairing up the lights and darks make 20 different combination sets. For each combination set you will need 4 - 5" light squares and 1 - 2 1/2" light strip AND 4 - 5" dark squares and 1 - 2 1/2" dark strip.

2. To make the four patch portions of the blocks, sew the light and dark 2 1/2" strips together, press seam to the dark fabric, and cut apart into 2 1/2" sections as shown. Then sew 8 four patch blocks from the cut 16 - 2 1/2" sections as shown below.

3. To make the half square triangle blocks, match a light 5" square (with a drawn diagonal line on back) with a dark 5" square. With right sides together stitch a seam 1/4" away from the drawn line on both sides of the drawn line. Cut apart on line and press to the dark fabric. Repeat with the remaining light and dark 5" squares of that color combination. Trim the resulting half square triangle blocks to 4 1/2".

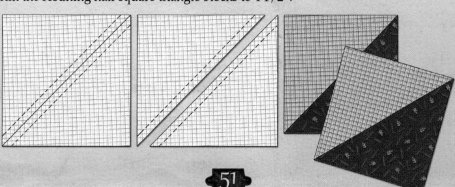

Market day in Brantôme

4. Using 8 four patch blocks and 8 half square triangle blocks in the same color combination, make the quilt block shown. Repeat to make the 19 remaining blocks.

5. Randomly arrange blocks in a way that is pleasing to you and sew quilt together.

6. Quilt as desired and bind. Binding directions can be found on page 53.

Binding:

In this method of binding, the binding is sewn to all four sides of the quilt and then the corners are done in the following way. This eliminates having to join the ends of the binding on a side of the quilt.

1. Fold binding strips in half length-wise, wrong sides together. Press.

2. Leaving at least 1 1/2" extra binding past each corner of the quilt, pin the folded binding strip to the quilt, raw edges together. With a 1/4" seam allowance, begin sewing 1/4" from the edge of the quilt, stop 1/4" from the other end of the quilt.

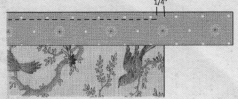

3. Press seam allowance toward binding. Pin the next folded binding strip into place, raw edges together. With a 1/4" seam allowance, begin stitching EXACTLY at the seam of the previous binding. THE STITCHES MUST MEET EXACTLY IN THE CORNERS.

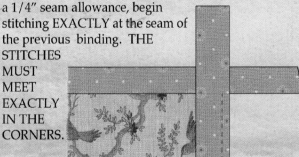

4. Once all four sides are sewn on, mark a square in the corners of the binding as shown. The sides of the squares should equal the distance from the seam to the folded edge of the binding. Draw two intersecting lines from corner to corner. Fold so that the folded edges of the bindings are lined up together.

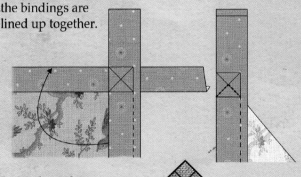

5. Stitch on the top two sides of the bottom triangle through both bindings. Trim away excess batting, backing and binding.

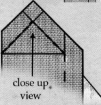

close up view

6. Fold the binding to the back taking care to turn the corners for a perfect miter. Hand stitch the binding to the back of the quilt.

Preparing Circles for Appliqué:

1. Cut a card stock circle the size you want your finished circle to be and cut your fabric circle about 3/8" larger all the way around than your card stock circle.

2. Run a line of gathering stitches close to the edge of your fabric circle and pull the gathered edges over the card stock circle. Tie gathering threads to hold gathers in place.

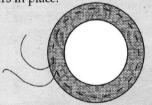

3. Spray gathered circle with starch and iron dry. Let circle cool completely (overnight is best if you have the time).

4. Clip the gathering thread just enough to remove the card stock circle. You do not have to remove the gathering thread if you do not want to. Now your perfect circle is ready to appliqué in place!

Felting Wool:

Felting wool is a very easy process. Be sure to look for 100% wool whether you are felting wool yardage you have purchased or old items of wool clothing you have found. Then, just wash the wool in hot water, rinse in cold, and dry in a hot dryer.

If you are using hand dyed wool, it has already been felted so you don't have to do a thing!

This is the view from the bell tower in Dinan. Just as we were admiring the bell it struck noon. It was a large (and loud) bell!

Fleur Press

As you roam the countryside, collect a flower here and there. With this miniature flower press you will be able to take a bit of France home with you. Write the name of the town the flower came from and you will have a lovely keepsake of your journey.

To make:

At your local hardware store purchase a strip of lumber 2 1/2" wide by 1/4" thick. These can be found in a variety of lengths. You can make some for gifts! Cut the wood into two 2 1/2" x 2 1/2" squares (front and back). Stain or paint all sides except for one side of one of the pieces. Copy the images below using a laser printer (your local print shop can do this for you, permission is given to copy this page for personal use). Loosely cut out the images. Using collage glue adhere the image to the unfinished side of the wood squares. The image will be larger than the wood. Let it dry. Using an exacto knife trim away the excess paper. Cut or tear several pieces of heavy watercolor paper slightly smaller than the wood pieces. Sandwich the paper between the wood and secure with an elastic hair band over two of the corners.

Flower baskets graced the streets along our way. September is a beautiful time of year to visit France.

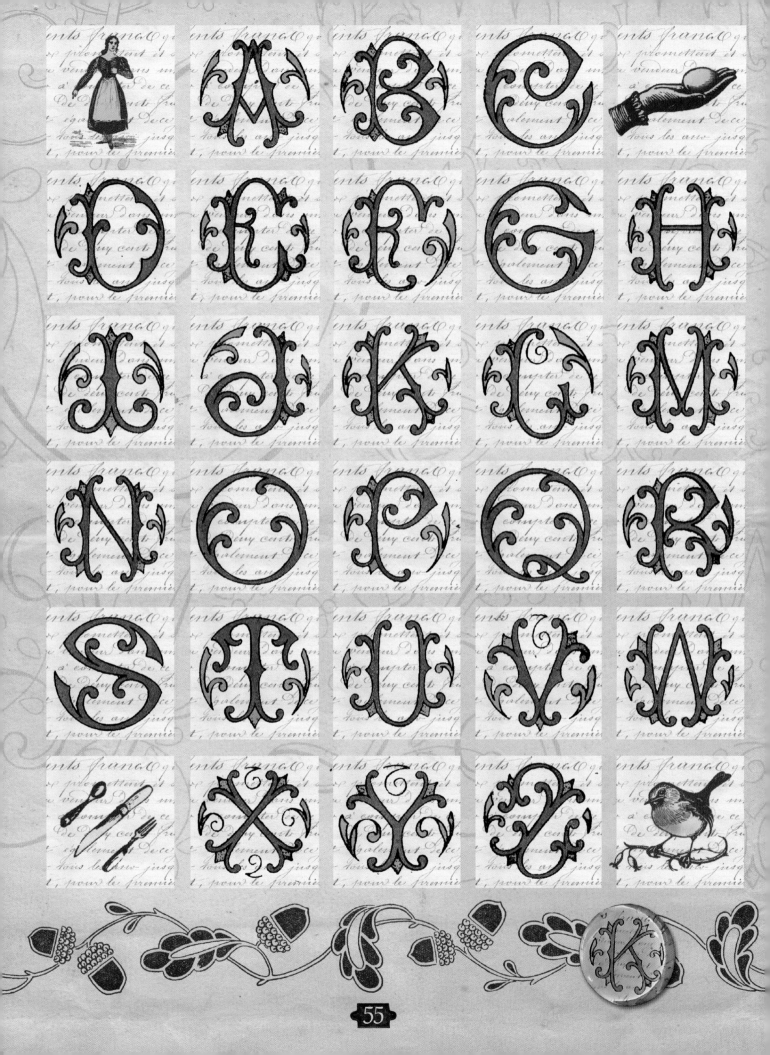

Souvenir Gardien

Souvenir Gardien

Red velvet token pillow designed by Bonnie Sullivan

Linen burlap token pillow designed by Kathy Schmitz

From Lille to Paris, the Flea Markets made our hearts beat a faster. Tiny treasures from long ago were quickly picked up by the fasted hands.
Our favorite French phrase ...

Combien pour tous? (How much for all?)

These Paris flea market display cushions were the inspiration for our very own token pillows.

opposite page

Soft velvet makes this token keeper appear instantly aged and loved. Cut 2 - 6" circles for the top and bottom. For the ruched edges cut a 2 1/2" x 40" strip. With right sides together, baste the two ends of the strip together using a 1/2" seam. Baste using a scant 1/4" seam on both sides of the strip loop. Gather to fit the 6" circle. With right sides together, using a 1/4" seam, sew the gathered strip to the top and bottom. Remove the basting stitches from the short end seam on the gathered strip. Turn right side out through this opening. Fill with crushed walnut shells (a funnel works well for this). Sew the opening closed.

Natural linen burlap and a linen ribbon are the base for this token keeper. Using rubber stamps, spell out the name and year of your adventure. Cut two pieces of linen sized to your token needs. With the ribbon sandwiched between the two, sew around all four sides leaving an opening for turning. The ribbon ends are sewn in the seams. Turn right side out, stuff, and stitch closed.

A little lavender fill will bring back memories of France.

Kathy's treasures

Simple Blessings

Simple Blessings 14" x 24"

designed by Bonnie Sullivan

Supplies:

Moda © 16" toweling - Flag Day Farm Red - 1 3/4 yard
Felted Wool pieces - pear gold, leaf green, pomegranate
light & dark red, urn light and dark brown, grape
lavender, bird blue & bird wing blue
Dark red wool (same as above) - 4 strips 3/4" x about 52"
Floss - The Gentle Art
     Sampler Threads - Soot #1050, Tarnished
       Gold #0410, Highland Heather #0830,
       Grecian Gold
     Simply Shaker - Berry Cobbler #7011,
       Harvest Basket #7000, Mountain Mist #7045
       Endive #7080, Parchment #7027,
       Pomegranate #7019
Pillow form 14" x 24" or stuffing
6 buttons - 1/4" black

Assembly:

The toweling for this project is 16" wide. Centering the red stripes, cut a 25" length of toweling trimming the width to 15". This piece is for the applique background. Again, centering the red stripes, cut 2 - 18" lengths which are also trimmed to 15" in width. These two pieces are for the back of the pillow. Using a large machine zigzag stitch, stitch around the outside edges of the three pieces to prevent raveling.

Using the pattern layout on the next page as a guide, arrange the urn, pomegranate, pear, grapes and bird on the background piece of toweling taking care to tuck pieces under or over others as indicated. Whip stitch the pieces in place using a coordinating color of thread. From your enlarged pattern mark the vines and stems. Using a stem stitch and 2 strands of Endive floss, embroider the vines and stems. Whip stitch the leaves and berries in place. Follow embroidery instructions on the following page to complete your pillow front.

Sew the 6 - 1/4" black buttons on to the center of the pomegranate using red thread as shown.

Fold over the ends of both of the pillow back pieces 2" and make two rows of top stitching on the folded edge - one row 1/4" in from the fold and another row 1 1/4" in from the fold as shown below.

With right sides together, and the folded ends of the two back pieces overlapping each other, sew around the entire pillow twice (for stability) using a 1/2" seam. Clip the corners, turn right side out and stuff with a 14" x 24" pillow form. If you do not have a pillow form that size, you will need to make one by cutting 2 - 15 1/2" x 25" pieces of muslin and, using a 1/2" seam allowance, make a pillow to stuff.

Cut 4 - 3/4" strips of deep red wool (the darker of the two reds used) across the width of the wool or about 52". Using a coordinating color of thread, run a basting thread down the center of the strips. Gather the strips to about 20" in length and machine stitch down the center of the gathered wool strips. Whip stitch the gathered wool strips around the edges of the pillow abutting the ends of the gathered strips together so there are no gaps. Cut off extra length of gathered wool if needed.

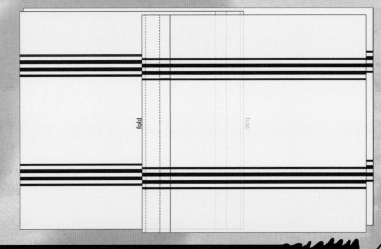

Gather wool strips for pillow trim.

Enlarge pattern 300% or enlarge the grid above to 1" squares (enlarged grid will be 21" x 10").
All striaght colored lines are stitched using a stem stitch. Around the pear and the stem use tarnished gold floss.
Berries are sewn on using a stroke stitch in pomegranate. Lavender is lazy daisy stitches in berry cobbler. The
bird's eye is a French knot in soot. For the bird legs use grecian gold. The pear seeds are done using a lazy daisy
stitch in the soot floss with another lazy daisy stitch in parchment floss inside of it. Vase accent highlights are
using harvest basket. Grape highlights are highland heather.

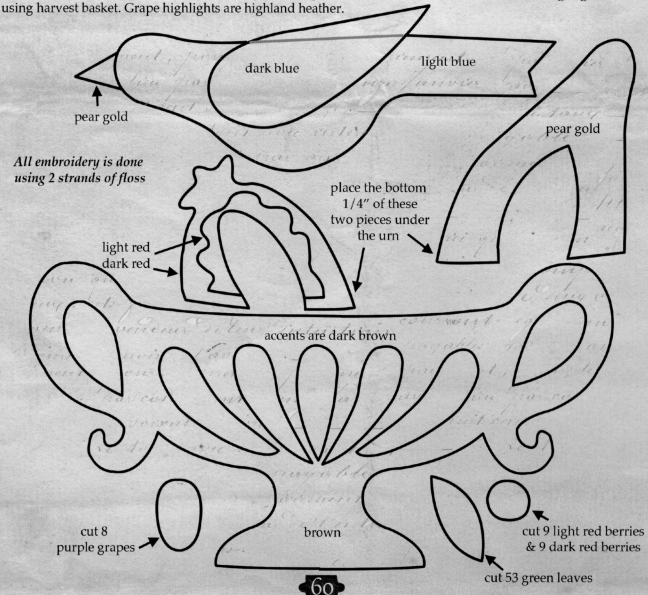

pear gold

dark blue

light blue

pear gold

*All embroidery is done
using 2 strands of floss*

place the bottom
1/4" of these
two pieces under
the urn

light red
dark red

accents are dark brown

cut 8
purple grapes

brown

cut 9 light red berries
& 9 dark red berries

cut 53 green leaves

Pin Coussin

Big or small, fancy or plain, you can never have enough pin cushions around. As you poke around the flea markets (or your cupboards) look at containers in a new light. We took antique silver pieces like creamers, sugar bowls, and even broken pocket watches, and gave them a new life.

To make:

Measure the diameter of the container you will be using. Cut a circle of velvet about twice that size. Run a line of basting stitches 1/4" in around the circle. Gather slightly and fill firmly with batting Pull the ends to gather tightly and tie off. Depending on the depth of you container, fill the bottom with crushed walnut shells for weight. This will require a bit of experimenting to find the right amount of fill. Stuff the velvet ball into the container with the gathered side to the bottom. Finagle the edges until they are smooth. (Yes, we said finagle in a sentence.)

Papier Weight

The paper images on pages on page 19 look trés joli placed behind a glass paper weight. Clear antique paper weights can be found at antique stores and new ones are readily available at craft stores and on-line. (See the resource guide on page 76.)

To make:

Find a paper weight blank to use. Place it over the image on page 19 you will be using. If the image size needs to be adjusted you will need to determine the correct size.
Have a laser copy printed of page 19.
Inkjet printer ink may smear with glue.
Permission is given to print that page for your personal use. If the image size needs to be adjusted, this is when you would make those changes. Place the paper weight over the printed image and trace around it. Cut it out slightly smaller than the paper weight. Using a collage medium, glue the image to the bottom of the weight. The finished piece may be backed with wool if desired.

La Chine

The French know how to relax and enjoy a cup of tea. This tea cozy will keep your teapot toasty & add a touch of ooh-la-la to your tea party.

La Chine *Tea Cozy 12" x 8"*

Designed by Kathy Schmitz

Supplies:

Light fabric - 14" x 10"
Print Backing fabric - 14" x 10"
Lining fabric - 14" X 20"
Binding fabric - 1/4 yard
Batting
Embroidery floss - The Gentle Art Sampler Threads
    Dark Chocolate #1170

Embroidery:

Trace the embroidery design onto the right side
of the light fabric, centered.

Stitch guide - 2 strands of thread used throughout
Teapot outline - Stem stitch
Teapot interior - Back stitch
Words - Stem stitch

*This sign in Honfleur was
the inspiration for this
teapot cozy*

Cutting & Assembly:

Trace the tea cozy pattern onto paper, flipping the design to complete the whole pattern. Cut it out on the drawn line. Place the pattern over the finished embroidery, with the design *centered* and cut out. Cut 1 piece of the backing fabric and 2 pieces of the lining fabric using the same pattern. Cut 2 pieces of batting from the same pattern. Sandwich a batting piece between the embroidery piece and one of the lining pieces, wrong sides together. Safety pin or baste them together. Machine quilt using diagonal cross hatch lines spaced 1" apart without quilting through the embroidery design. Do the same thing with the backing fabric, lining piece, and batting.

From the extra lining fabric cut one piece 3 1/2" long and 2" wide. Fold right sides together and stitch along the 3 1/2" side using a 1/4" seam. Turn right side out and press so that the seam runs down the center. Fold in half to form a loop.

Sew the front to the back with the linings facing each other using a scant 1/4" seam.

From the binding fabric cut 2 strips 2 1/2" by width of fabric. Press these in half lengthwise with wrong sides together.
Pin the raw ends of the lining fabric loop (from above) matching up with the center of the back of the cozy. Sew the binding onto the *embroidered* side of the cozy body as you would a quilt. Hand stitch the folded edge of the binding to the back of the cozy.

Sew the remaining binding piece around the bottom of the cozy starting and stopping on the back side of the cozy.

Tack the loop to the binding so that it will stand straight up.

1/2 of the teapot pattern - flip it over to complete the full pattern

This is 1/2 of the pattern; Complete the pattern by flipping this half over. After you have made the complete pattern -
Cut 1 of light fabric for embroidery
Cut 1 of backing fabric
Cut 2 of lining fabric

1

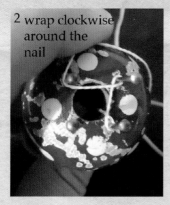
2 wrap clockwise around the nail

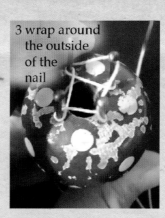
3 wrap around the outside of the nail

4 pull the loop on the bottom over the top thread and nail.

French Knitting Antique Button Necklace

Designed by Kathy Schmitz

When we were kids we called this spool knitting, but in France they take ownership of this old-fashioned past time. Bonnie found this sweet wooden mushroom "spool" at an antique shop called Grenier de Brantôme in Brantôme, France. It brought back wonderful memories for both of us and we had to have it. If you don't have an antique mushroom spool don't fret! You can make your own by using an old wooden spool and four small nails. You will need 8 wt Perle cotton in a color of your choice. I used Ecru to match my antique buttons. You will also need a small crochet hook, I used a number 4. Start by threading the perle cotton through the spool. Follow the steps above. Tug on the bottom thread often. Make knitted cord as long as you would like. Mine is 18". The weight of the buttons will stretch the cording a little. Once you have knitted the length you want, simply cut the Perle cotton leaving a nice long end. Thread this end through the loops and cast off of the nails. Pull the thread tight and

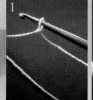
1

2

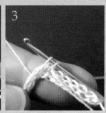
3

4 pull through both loops

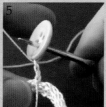
5

6

7

single crochet one end so it is long enough to form a loop and then secure it hiding the end by threading it back through the cording. On the other end, sew a button and hide that thread the same way. Starting about 2" from one end insert the crochet hook through the thickest part of the knitted tube (see above). Make 3 single crochet stitches and

then add a button. Make 3 single crochet stitches and slip the crochet hook through the thickest part of the knitted tube about 1/4" from where you began. Continue adding buttons using this method. Place the smaller buttons near the ends with the larger buttons nearer to the middle of the necklace. You may also choose to differ the lengths of the single crochet stitches so that the buttons hang at different lengths. Keep the same number of stitches on either side of a button. Weave loose threads through the center of the knitted tube.

For novice spool knitter's, how-to videos can be found on YouTube.

Acorn Manor

Acorn Manor
Table Topper 47 1/2" x 47 1/2"

Designed by Kathy Schmitz
Quilted by Laurel Keith / Hawn Creek Quilting

The directions for the appliqué table topper are for fusible web, raw edge appliqué. If you wish to appliqué using the turned method, additional yardage may be needed.

Supplies:
1 1/8 yard - Light appliqué background fabric
1 yard - Dark green fabric for stems and leaves
10" x 10" - Light green fabric for acorns
8"x 8" + 1/8 yard- Dark red fabric for acorn tops & for inside border
1 1/8 yard - Focal print for outside border and center fussy cut
Fusible web - 2 1/3 - 2 1/2 yards from a 12" wide roll
Batting
Freezer paper

Cutting:
Cut the appliqué background fabric to a 34 1/2" square
Dark green fabric - (see diagram below)
  Cut 5 strips 2 1/4" by width of fabric for binding
  Cut 2 strips 1" x 34 1/2" for inside border
  Cut 2 strips 1" x 35 1/2" for inside border
  Set aside the remainder of the dark green for the appliqué
Dark red fabric -
  Cut 4 strips 1" by width of fabric for the inside border
Focal print fabric -
  Cut 5 strips 6" by width of fabric

Unbelievable mosaic tiled floors graced the floors in many of the churches. This one was the inspiration for Acorn Manor.

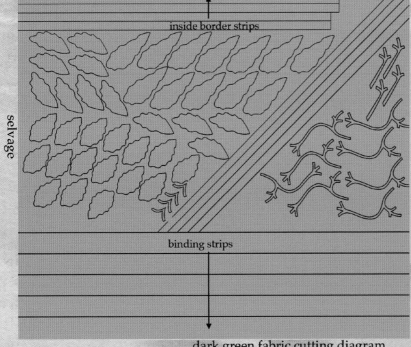

inside border strips

selvage

selvage

binding strips

dark green fabric cutting diagram

Appliqué:
On a 1 1/2" x 36" piece of the fusible web, draw 5 lines 1/4" apart. Iron this to the wrong side of the dark green fabric on the BIAS following the manufacturer's directions (see diagram above). Cut out the strips on the a drawn lines for a total of 4 - 1/4" wide BIAS strips.
For the remainder of the green pieces, trace appliqué patterns onto the fusible web leaving a small amount around each shape. Using the above diagram for placement, iron the fusible web to the wrong side of the fabric following the manufacturer's directions. Cut the pieces out on the lines.
Cut out the acorns and acorn caps using this same method in their fabrics.

Find the centers of the center light appliqué background piece - horizontally, vertically, and diagonally. Baste along each of these lines following the diagram below. Cut the 4 - 1/4" wide green appliqué strips to 21" in lengths.

Do this step next.

Trace this shape onto a piece of freezer paper keeping the shape away from the edges by at least 1" (see below). Cut out the shape from the center of the freezer paper without cutting through the outside border of the paper (A). Use this template as a window to find the section of fabric you would like to fussy cut. Iron the freezer paper to the *right* side of the fabric. Iron a piece of fusible web to the wrong side of the fabric. Cut out the fabric using the freezer paper negative space as your pattern. Iron this fussy cut piece, with the webbing on the back side, to the center of the light background fabric matching up the points with the diagonal basting lines.

A

Start placing the long vines following the diagrams below. The vines start about 7 1/2" from the outside corner, then follow the diagonal basting lines until it meets the fussy cut piece. Follow these curves overlapping the fussy cut fabric by 1/8" and continue up the next diagonal line. *Do not iron the vines in place yet*, just stick them temporarily. Arrange all four of the main vines.

Start placing the other vines along the main vine following the diagrams below. Trim where overlapped as needed.

Once all of the vines are in place start adding the leaves and acorns. This will take some maneuvering until they are in a position that works for you. When all of the pieces are in place, iron the appliqué pieces following the manufacturer's directions. Remove any visible basting stitches.

The raw edges of the appliqué pieces will be sewn down during quilting.

stitch basting lines - horizontal, vertical and diagonal

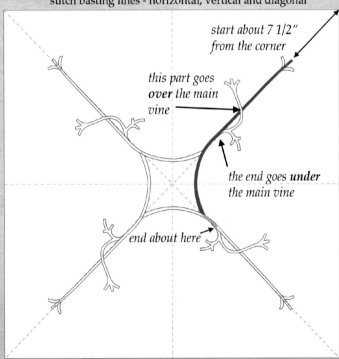

start about 7 1/2" from the corner

this part goes *over* the main vine

the end goes *under* the main vine

end about here

use some of the leftover vine pieces for these 4 short stems

Assembly: all seams are 1/4"

Sew the 2 green strips 1" x 34 1/2" to the sides of the appliqué center piece. Press toward the green. Sew the 2 green strips 1" x 35 1/2" to the sides. Press toward the green. Trim the green to 1/2" all the way around.

Measure through the vertical center of the piece. Cut 2 of the red 1" strips to this length. Sew these to the sides. Press toward the red. Measure through the horizontal center of the piece. Cut the other 2 red 1" strips to this length. Sew these to the top and the bottom. Press toward the red. Trim the red to 1/2" all the way around.

Wide outside border:
Measure through the vertical center of the piece. Cut 2 of the focal print fabric strips to this length. Sew these 2 strips to the sides of the piece. Press toward the outside border. Using a 5/8" seam, sew the remaining 3 strips together to form one long strip. Measure through the horizontal center of the table topper and cut 2 strips to that length from the pieced border strip. Sew them to the top and the bottom. Press toward the outside border.

Quilt and bind. Binding directions are on page 53.

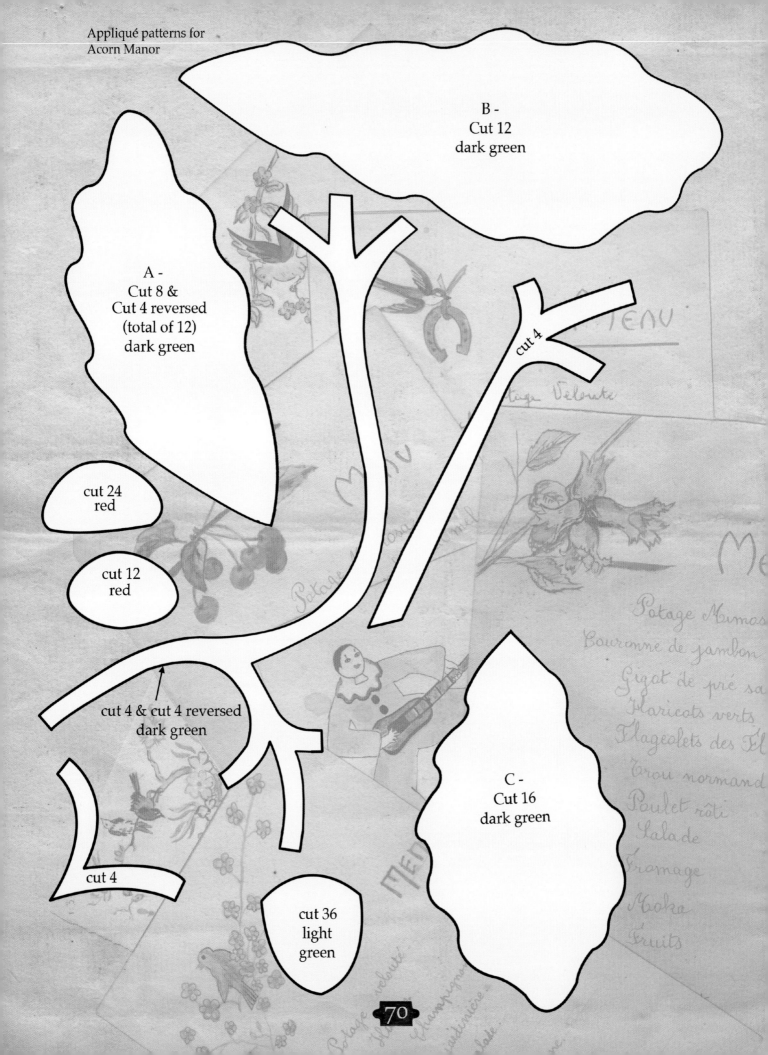

B -
Cut 12
dark green

A -
Cut 8 &
Cut 4 reversed
(total of 12)
dark green

cut 4

cut 24
red

cut 12
red

cut 4 & cut 4 reversed
dark green

cut 4

C -
Cut 16
dark green

cut 36
light
green

Garden Charm

Garden Charm 13" x 17"
Designed by Bonnie Sullivan

If you made the Ville De Paris quilt featured on page 6 and you sewed the extra seam while making the snowballed blocks, then you should have ended up with 96 small half square triangle blocks. Press these blocks with the seams open and trim them to 1 1/2" square. If you will be making this piece without the pre made blocks, the supply list follows on page 75.

Supplies: In addition to the above half square triangle blocks you will also need:

 Red (same as the half square triangles) - 1/8 yard (not a fat 1/8)

 Light stripe - 7 1/2" x 11 1/2" (appliqué background)

Appliqué fabric - green 8" x 10, brown 6" x 4", 2 reds - scraps
Backing fabric of your choice - fat quarter
Buttons - 5 - 1/2" ivory
Fusible web
Floss - The Gentle Arts Sampler Thread Cinnamon #0510
         The Gentle Arts Simply Shaker Pomegranate #7019, Endive #7080

The gardens of Château Villandry, situated in the Loire Valley, inspired this petite patchwork wall hanging.

Cutting:
From the Red fabric:
Cut 3 - 1" strips by the width of the fabric
Cut the strips as follows - 2 - 1" x 8 1/2", 2 - 1" x 11 1/2", 2 - 1" x 13 1/2", and 2 - 1" x 16 1/2" for the borders
From the backing fabric:
Cut 2 - 7 1/4" x 17 1/2" pieces

Assembly: Appliqué is applied after the border is sewn on. Sew the small quilt together as shown. Stay stitch a scant 1/4" in from the edges on all four sides.

Appliqué:
Trace the appliqué patterns onto the fusible web following the manufacturers directions. Cut the pieces out leaving extra around each piece (do not cut them out on the traced line). Remove the paper backing from the fusible web. Stick the fusible web pieces to the wrong side of the corresponding fabric to be used. Iron according to the web directions. Cut out the pieces on the traced lines. Following the guide on the next page, beginning with the background pieces first, arrange the appliqué pieces onto the center of the appliqué background fabric, 1/2" from the bottom and 1" from the top. Iron the pieces in place. Using the endive floss chain stitch around the stems and leaves. Using the pomegranate floss whip stitch around the flowers. Button hole in cinnamon around the urn.

flower patterns

Backing:

Using a 1/2" seam, with right sides together, sew the two backing pieces as shown. ***Use a basting stitch between the two dots.*** Press the seam open.

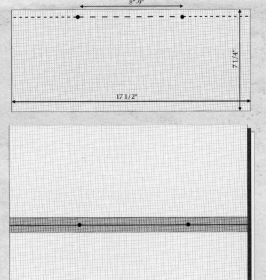

Place the quilt back and the applique top right sides together. Place a 13 1/2" x 16 1/2" piece of batting on the back side of the quilt top as shown. Using a 1/4" seam allowance sew completely around the small quilt through all three layers. Clip corners. Open the seam in the center of the backing where the basting stitches are. Turn the quilt right side out. Press the quilt and sew the opening in the backing closed.

Quilt as desired. Sew the buttons on across the top of the urn. To frame, we covered a piece of heavy cardboard (16" x 20") with old music sheets and coated it with a collage medium. The small quilt is attached to the center of the cardboard. By poking holes through the cardboard, behind the corners of the quilt, it can then be sewn on with a needle and thread. Catch only the back of the quilt fabric so the stitches won't show on the front. Insert the cardboard into the frame.

If you did not make the Ville de Paris quilt on page 6 and therefore do not have the 96 small half square triangle blocks needed for this project, you will have to make them using the additional fabric and directions listed here:

3/8 yard of main red print
Cut 3 - 2 1/2" strips across width of fabric. Cut 2 1/2" strips into 48 - 2 1/2" squares.
Cut 3 - 1" strips across width of fabric. Cut 1" strips into 2 - 1" x 16 1/2" strips, 2 - 1" x 13 1/2" strips, 2 - 1" x 11 1/2" strips, and 2 - 1" x 8 1/2" strips for the borders.

A fat 1/8th yard (10 1/2" x 18" with stripes running the long direction) of the striped fabric
Cut 1 - 7 1/2" x 11 1/2" piece of the striped fabric for the background of the applique center.
Cut 4 - 2 1/2" squares for half square triangle blocks.

A 6" square of each of the 12 fabrics shown.
From each fabric: Cut 4 - 2 1/2" squares.

You will need a fat quarter of a fabric of your choice for backing.

To make the half square triangle blocks:
Match each red 2 1/2" square with a 2 1/2" square of a different fabric. Draw a diagonal line on the back of one of the 2 1/2" squares in each pair. Sew a seam on both sides of the drawn line, 1/4" away from the line. Cut apart on drawn line. Press seams open and trim sewn blocks to 1 1/2" square.

Follow the directions on page 73 to complete the small quilt.

Resources & Floss Conversion

Craft supplies -

Glass paper weights - www.sierrapacificcrafts.org for a store location near you
Pendant blanks - Darice® *Signed, Sealed & Remembered* .63" x 1.57" frame charm rectangle silver. Check with your local craft store

Machine Quilters:

Laurel Keith / Hawn Creek Quilting Hawn.Creek.quilting@frontier.com
Pam Parvin / Kay Lee Quilting
Loretta Orsborn / Orsborn Specialty Quilting www.orsbornequilting.com

Hand Dyed Wools:

Blackberry Primitives www.blackberryprimitives.com
Mary Flanigan www.mfwoolens.com
Gina Conway Hand-dyed Wool & What-Not's - wool available through www.PioneerQuiltshop.com

Jewelry:

Ann Fenderson / Next Chapter Jewelry www.etsy.com/shop/nextchapterjewelry

Floss Conversion Chart

The Gentle Arts Sampler Threads to DMC

Grecian gold	DMC #680
Dark Chocolate #1170	DMC #839
Highland Heather #0830	DMC #3042
Old Brick #0320	DMC #760
Raspberry Parfait #0380	DMC #3831
Cranberry #0360	DMC #902
Cinnamon #0510	DMC #300
Soot #1050	DMC #844
Willow #0160	DMC #3012
Onyx #7063	DMC Black
Tarnished Gold #0410	DMC #167

Simply Shaker

Crystal Lake #7075	DMC #413
Toffee #7078	DMC #3829
Harvest Basket #7000	DMC #612
Lexington Green #7040	DMC #3023
Parchment #7027	DMC #3782
Piney Woods #7082	DMC #3781 & #730 (one strand of each)
Mountain Mist #7045	DMC #926
Toasted Barley #7064	DMC #642
Endive #7080	DMC #3012
Pomegranate #7019	DMC #3721
Berry Cobbler #7011	DMC #3836

A great source for all kinds of antiques and treasures is the annual flea market in Lille, France. This special event is held the first weekend of September (which is why we took our trip then). It is Europe's largest flea market! The streets were closed to make room for thousands of vendors. And if you like moules & frites (mussels and fries) this is where you want to be! The restaurants have contests to see which one serves the most. Don't forget to try a "real" Belgium Waffle for dessert!

We met many angels on the trip who made our journey so very memorable and sometimes quite literally helped us find our way.

Christel & Raymond

We want to thank Valerie for helping us the first morning when we arrived at Charles de Gaulle Airport in Paris. What do you do if the kiosk where you're trying to buy train tickets to Brugge doesn't accept your American credit card and doesn't want to sell you a ticket all the way to Brugge, but only to Lille? We were holding up the line and sweet Valerie graciously stepped in and bought our tickets (we gave her Euros of course!), took us to the right train, and got us on our way. We realize you may never see this book, but what a blessing you were to us that day!

Christel, and her father Raymond, met us the next morning and gave us a tour of the beautiful town of Brugge (sometimes referred to as "The Venice of the North"). The day ended with a trip to Raymond's favorite chocolate shop where he bought us both a box of the most exquisite Belgian chocolates. Can you say YUMMM!!!!!! We met Christel at Quilt Market and she has a wonderful shop near Ghent called, 't Dreefhuys. Thank you, thank you Christel and Raymond!

Dumon Chocolates!

We also met with Christina, owner of Paprika Cotton, a quilt shop in Tournai, Belgium. She is another shop owner we met at Quilt Market and was gracious enough to show us around her beautiful store. Thank you Christina!

In Dinan we met Nadine. We invited her to share our table at a little bistro across the street from where we were doing our laundry. She spoke as much English as we did French, but somehow we found a way to communicate with a notepad, pen, and pictures. She let us know what would be good to order for our lunch and spent an hour or so with us in good attempts at conversation. It was a lovely time. Again, Nadine will probably never see this book but we want to thank her!

Christina

We met with Carol, in Nantes and she showed us around Quiltmania and introduced us to her staff. What a treat! Bonnie and Carol discussed the progress of the book Bonnie was doing with Quiltmania called, "Bonnie's Garden" (which has now been published - shameless plug). We told Carol where we were headed after our visit and she even went online and found a place for us to stay the night and made dinner reservations in the town we were headed to as we wouldn't be getting in until late. You're an angel Carol!

The next part of our trip took us to the Dordogne region of France which is stunningly gorgeous and was one of our favorite places. We ended up in the little village of Beynac and went about looking for a place to stay. As there were only a couple to choose from it didn't take too long, but our decision was easily made as soon as we were greeted by Hilda. Hilda's warmth and sense of humor made us feel as though we had know her forever. Thank you Hilda for being the lovely person you are and making us feel so at home.

As you can see we felt so blest to have met these wonderful people on our journey. They each helped to make our trip just as memborable as the sights we took in. A hearfelt thanks to you one and all.

This is a rooftop garden in Brugge. An amazing little city surrounded by a canal. You will need a full day to explore this gem. Climb the bell tower for the best view. You will see all of the "Brugge Red" rooftops.

For the BEST chocolate in Belgium, stop by Dumon for a box of their delicious, and beautiful, chocolates! We even took a picture of them before we ate them (page 77).

The Lille flea market enveloped the whole city center. What a treasure trove – something for everyone! Looking for a button? A toy sewing machine? You will find it in Lille the first weekend of September! (Keep in mind there will be 2 million others there with you.)

Dinan was a lovely place to stay for a couple of days. Weave your way down the narrow streets and you will find something beautiful around every corner.

Brantôme was a sweet little city with many good restaurants overlooking the small river that ran through the town. We found a huge antique shop situated inside of a cave. It was nice and cool inside, and a little damp, but it was also filled to the brim with old linens, laces, jewelry, glass odds and ends, old papers, buttons and about anything else you could think off.

Bonnie found some neat papers

This is the view while floating down the Dordogne River. Just around the corner is Beynac - a great place to stay.

Fabulous antique store we found on our way to Beynac. A quick U-turn and we were in antique heaven!

Kathy found an old book

A Paris flea market......treasures! Take a pen & paper with you to communicate about prices. "Fifty" sounds an awful lot like "Fifteen" with a heavy French accent!

Kathy found this sweet etching at the flea market. If you look closely at the cover of this book, you will recognize this etching as the background. Part of this etching is also offered as a pendant image on page 19.

La Fin